TRANQUILLITY
& INSIGHT

AN INTRODUCTION TO THE OLDEST
FORM OF BUDDHIST MEDITATION

Amadeo Solé-Leris

Shambhala
Boston
1986

SHAMBHALA PUBLICATIONS, INC.
314 DARTMOUTH STREET
BOSTON, MASSACHUSETTS 02116

Library of Congress Cataloging-in-Publication Data
Solé-Leris, Amadeo.
  Tranquillity & insight.

  Bibliography: p.
  Includes index.
  1. Śamatha (Buddhism) 2. Vipaśyanā (Buddhism)
3. Meditation (Buddhism) I. Title. II. Title:
Tranquillity and insight.
BQ5612.S65 1986   294.3′443   86-11834
ISBN 0-87773-385-6 (pbk.)

TRANQUILLITY
& INSIGHT

Contents

Preface

The practice of meditation is the heart of the Buddha's teaching. This book aims therefore to achieve two things. First, to sketch an outline of Buddhist meditation according to the oldest tradition and as a living practice in our time. This is intended to serve as a general introduction to the subject for the non-specialized reader which may, it is hoped, encourage him or her to have a try (chapters 1, 2, 3, 7 and 8).

The second purpose is to offer a survey of the meditational techniques involved (chapters 4, 5, 6 and 9). This, while very compressed, goes into sufficient detail to serve also – together with the references given in the Notes and the Selected Bibliography – as a simple manual which the interested reader can use as a starting point for further study.

Some readers may at first wish to go rather quickly through the more technical chapters and come back to them for more details when they have rounded out the general picture. Others may, from the beginning, prefer to follow the progressively unfolding design of the book, each chapter leading into the next. Either way, this book will have served its purpose if it helps to promote a better appreciation of the direct, practical nature of the Buddha's teaching.

1
Introduction

All meditative traditions, whatever the differences in underlying belief systems and in specific techniques, agree in one essential respect: the cause of the dissatisfaction, anxiety and suffering which seem to be inseparable from our lives lies in a basic misinterpretation of the true nature of existence, a misinterpretation which clouds our perception of the actual facts, in consequence of which we persist in futile attempts to pursue and secure things (such as health, riches, happiness and so on) which are, by their very nature, ephemeral or unattainable. We seem to be swimming constantly against the current.

Meditative traditions also agree that, to overcome this state of affairs, neither intellectual understanding nor religious faith are, in themselves, enough. Something must be *done*. Not only outwardly, by performing acts of charity or of devotion (however beneficial these may be in helping others and in improving the mental attitude of the doer), but inwardly: each person needs to work on him or herself to correct the fundamentally distorted perception of reality. This working on oneself, this internal reorganization of the psyche, is meditation.

The purpose of the present study of Buddhist meditation is to offer a general view – inevitably rather abbreviated, but complete in essentials – of the methods of meditation which were tried out, perfected and taught by that great master, the Buddha, some 2500 years ago, as they have been preserved in the most ancient traditions of his teaching. We know those meditative techniques in detail thanks to the texts of the Pali canon,[1] which have preserved the words of the Buddha, and also through the living transmission of meditation practice, handed down from generation to generation in the oldest unbroken tradition of

9

Buddhism, known as Theravāda (in Pali, *theravāda* means the doctrine, or teaching, of the elders), which lives on today in the countries of Southeast Asia (mainly Sri Lanka, Burma and Thailand).[2]

Over the centuries, as Buddhism developed and spread both in India, its homeland, and in many other parts of Asia – Tibet, China, Japan, the islands of Nusantara (now Indonesia), and so on – various branches of what is known as Mahāyāna Buddhism evolved and flourished. These, while not differing in essentials (since they are all, like Theravāda, anchored in the teachings of the historical Buddha), are characterized by complex elaborations and accretions of a religious, philosophical and cultural nature, which are also reflected in their own meditative techniques.

These cannot be dealt with in this study, and so we must leave aside, for example, the rich and varied visualizations and mentations of Tibetan Buddhism, the deliberate paradoxes of koans, or the 'just sitting' practice *(shikan-taza)* of the Soto school of Zen (which is a pure type of insight meditation and, as such, the closest to *vipassanā* in its original form). However, anyone who is at all familiar with these other techniques will immediately realize, on reading the following pages, that they all have, to a greater or lesser extent, their roots in the methods of mental concentration described in chapter 4 below, and that they are related to one or the other of the two main branches of Buddhist meditation defined in chapter 3 and discussed at length in chapters 5, 6 and 9: *samatha* – tranquillity meditation, or *vipassanā* – insight meditation.

There are two reasons (apart from the practical limitations of available time and space) why this study focuses deliberately on the earliest forms of Buddhist meditation. The first is the desire to foster a better knowledge and understanding of the sources of the varied range of later Buddhist meditation practices (some of which, such as Zen, have aroused considerable interest in the West). The second, and much more important, reason is the firm conviction that Buddhist meditation in its most unvarnished, original form is of particular relevance to our times and can prove especially useful and beneficial in coping with the turmoil of the modern world. The thoroughly pragmatic nature of the Buddha's teaching, with its absence of dogma, makes a particularly potent appeal in this day and age to those, and there are many, who are tired and suspicious of the conflicting claims of so many different 'isms', religious, philosophical and doctrinal.

To start with, it should be made clear at once that Buddhism is not, in effect, an 'ism'. The word 'Buddhism' itself is a term coined, and originally used, by non-Buddhists as a convenient label. 'Buddhists' themselves speak, more accurately, of following and practising the *Buddha Sāsana* and the *Buddha Dhamma*, the doctrine and teaching of the Enlightened One, a teaching whose heart is, precisely, the practice of meditation. This is so because of the concrete and practical character of this teaching, which deliberately leaves aside metaphysical and theological considerations to concentrate on what each one of us can and needs to do himself (since no human or superhuman power can do it for another), here and now, to clarify and reorganize his mental processes so as to gain the full and accurate experience of the true nature of things, i.e. of what philosophers like to call 'reality'.

'Buddhist' meditation (to go on using the label for convenience's sake) does not mean, therefore, that one has to start by blindly accepting certain beliefs before one may practise it or that one must perform specific rituals or ceremonies on which the effectiveness of the meditation itself might depend.[3] It means, quite simply, to practise the techniques of mental training tried out and taught by the Buddha himself, which do not demand a preliminary commitment to an organized religion. To illustrate this fundamental aspect, let me quote from the *Code of Discipline* which is placed in the hands of each new student attending a modern teaching centre of *vipassanā* meditation:

The entire Path (Dhamma) is a universal remedy for universal problems, and has nothing to do with any organized religion or sectarianism. For this reason, it can be practised freely by all, without conflict with race, caste or religion, in any place, at any time and will prove equally beneficial to one and all.[4]

The essential characteristic of this teaching and this tradition is to place every person squarely face to face with his or her own responsibilities. Of course, anyone who wishes to practise these meditation techniques as taught by the Buddha needs guidance and instruction. The would-be meditator, like anyone wishing to learn any technique or discipline in any field of human activity, needs a teacher to guide him and explain things to him. But the teacher is just that: someone who, having acquired specific knowledge and skills, is now concerned with passing them on to others. What a Buddhist teacher most definitely is not is an intercessor, a middleman between the uninitiated and some divine power; nor is he a wonderworker, or a human manifestation of some kind of divinity. There is no salvation through grace, no salvation through faith; nor are there go-betweens of any kind. The Buddha's injunctions – in this as in everything else – were perfectly simple and clear:

11

That which I have proclaimed and made known as the Teaching and the Rule, that shall be your Master when I am gone. . . .

Be ye an island unto yourselves, a refuge unto yourselves, seeking no external refuge; with the Teaching as your island, the Teaching your refuge, seeking no other refuge.[5]

This is how the Buddha exhorted his disciples shortly before his final passing away. And his rightly famous last words were:

Behold now, monks, I exhort you, transient are all the elements of being. Strive with earnestness![6]

These few words may at first appear rather cryptic but, in fact, they summarize with admirable concision the essence of the Buddha's teaching.

First of all one has to face up to the real dilemma without the usual equivocations and procrastinations: the transience of 'all the elements of being'. That is to say, one has to come to grips with the fact that absolutely everything that makes up this shifting, manifold universe that we experience with our senses and our minds is transient, ephemeral. Everything sooner or later decays, changes and disappears, including ourselves. And it is because of our deeply ingrained reluctance to face the full implications of this all too obvious fact that we persist in wanting to hold on to the things we value – pleasure, health, wealth, happiness, life itself – while they slip inevitably through our fingers. We yearn for a stability and permanence which cannot be found anywhere in the world, and it is this unsatisfied yearning that generates the characteristic anxiety of the unenlightened human condition.

Obviously, once one has recognized this fact intellectually, the next step is to see how to get out of this impossible situation. The Buddha's solution does not consist in consoling oneself with hopes of a blissful and eternal hereafter (which does not do away with desire and yearning, but simply replaces present objects in this life with a hypothetical object later on), but in doing something specific here and now, by working on ourselves by means of the mental training techniques which he himself perfected, i.e. by practising meditation. This is the task at which we have to 'strive with earnestness'. This is the concrete, active nature of the Buddha's message, which he stressed time and again, for instance, in the simple yet moving closing words of the last sermon in the *Majjhima Nikāya* (*Collection of Middle-Length Discourses*):

See here these trees, see here these solitary spots. Meditate, and do not be remiss, that you may not have cause to regret it later. This is my advice to you.[7]

2
Buddha Dhamma –
The Buddha's Teaching

1 The first point to bear in mind is that the heart of the Buddha's teaching is the practice of meditation. In other words, this is a *practical* teaching about what one can do to improve matters in concrete terms; it is not an exercise in metaphysical speculation or theological construction. The Buddha made the point forcefully in his famous parable of the poisoned arrow:

Suppose someone comes along and says: 'I will not lead the life of purity that the Blessed One teaches unless he first tells me whether the world is eternal or not, whether it is finite or infinite; whether body and soul are one and the same, or two different things; whether the Perfect One will endure after death, or will not endure, or whether he will both endure and not endure, or whether he will neither endure nor not endure.' Such a one will certainly die long before the Perfect One can explain all this to him.

It is as if a man were wounded by a poisoned arrow, and his companions, friends and relatives had sent for a surgeon to treat him, and the injured man were to say: 'Oh no! I don't want the arrow pulled out until I know who has wounded me: whether he is a noble warrior, a brahmin, a commoner or a servant; what his name is, and his family, whether he is tall, medium or small. . . .' Most certainly, such a man would perish before they could answer his questions. Similarly, if one refuses to lead the life of purity before he has had all these questions answered about whether the world is or is not eternal, and all the rest, he will certainly die before the Perfect One can explain all this to him.

'The world is eternal', 'the world is not eternal' . . . all these are just views and opinions . . . but what is certain is that there is birth, old age and death, that there is sorrow and lamentation, pain, grief and tribulation, and what I teach you is how to do away with all this in this very life.[8]

13

2 One has to be practical. But, of course, even while avoiding theories and unnecessary speculations, communication between human beings cannot take place without a minimum of conceptual and verbal activity. To teach someone to do something, you have to start by giving him at least a general idea of what it is all about, of what he will be trying to do, and of how to do it. The Buddha, too, had to develop some instructions, some verbal teaching in which he formulated, in the simplest possible terms, the understanding he had achieved of the human condition and of the way to overcome its shortcomings by means of a determined effort which commits all the resources of the human mind to the task of achieving the total integration of *nibbāna* (nirvana).[9]

In order to place the meditative techniques, which are discussed later, in their proper context, it is therefore necessary to have in one's mind a clear outline of the Buddha's teaching, the *Buddha Dhamma*, which he summarized in his first sermon on the 'Four Noble Truths', preached at Isipatana (modern Sarnath, near Varanasi) some two months after his own definitive enlightenment. Even though these Four Noble Truths might be taken as generally known, since they have been quoted, explained and commented upon on innumerable occasions, it will be helpful to recapitulate them before proceeding further.

3 *The Four Noble Truths*

These are:

the Truth of Suffering
the Truth of the Origin of Suffering
the Truth of the Cessation of Suffering
the Truth of the Way leading to the Cessation of Suffering

3.1 *Suffering (*dukkha*)*

Birth is suffering, ageing is suffering, death is suffering; sorrow, lamentation, pain, grief and tribulation are suffering; association with what one dislikes is suffering; separation from what one likes is suffering; not to get what one wants is suffering.[10]

It is important to bear in mind that the Pali term *dukkha*, which is usually translated as 'suffering', has a much broader range of connotation in the original. It includes not only acute or manifest states of mental or physical suffering, but also any degree of unpleasantness, discomfort, dissatisfaction, anxiety or unease. It may be noted in this

14

connection that the Venerable Nyānatiloka's *Buddhist Dictionary* specifies that it 'refers to the unsatisfactory nature and the general insecurity of all conditioned phenomena' and suggests that, were it not for stylistic reasons, ' "unsatisfactoriness" or "liability to suffering" would be more adequate renderings'.

It must be quite clear that this first truth does not deny the existence of pleasurable experiences, but simply draws attention to the fact that, even in the midst of pleasure and happiness, we are never free from some discomfort or unease for any length of time. Pleasures are fleeting, happiness is ephemeral (as not only the Buddha but all religious teachers and philosophers are ever reminding us), and their enjoyment, if at all clear-headed, is tinged with this knowledge. What is more, if we pay close attention, how often can we say in the course of ordinary, everyday existence that we are enjoying a moment of perfect, unalloyed happiness or comfort? How often can we say that we are entirely free from everything we dislike, that we have everything we like, that the constant, complex weaving of our desires is entirely stilled? And how often does it happen (to take banal, but for all that significant, examples) that one feels an itch in one's nose, or that one's foot has gone to sleep, or the sun gets in one's eyes, or one remembers the unpaid electricity bill, just in the middle of an otherwise rapturous experience?

Unease, in the full sense of the term, is universal: we are not, in any lasting sense, at ease in the world as we experience it; we are not at ease in ourselves. It is therefore true to say that, looked at without illusions, *to live is to suffer*. All philosophies and religions agree on the condition. Disagreement begins when it comes to analysing the causes of this unease and to finding remedies for it. Here the Buddha's answer is remarkable for its simplicity and directness: *to suffer is to want*, i.e. to need and therefore desire, something one does not have.

3.2 *The Origin of Suffering* (dukkha samudaya)

In fact, the origin of all this suffering, discomfort and unease is 'craving, which leads to rebirth and is accompanied by pleasure and desire, taking pleasure in this and that.'[11]

The full import of this statement, oversimplified though it may seem at first, becomes clear as soon as one considers that the pursuit of pleasure is, in fact, a very comprehensive activity. It is motivated not only by desire for what one likes but also by aversion for what one dislikes, since aversion is only a 'desire to avoid' whatever is perceived as unpleasant or undesirable. A moment's reflection will show how much of our time and energy we spend throughout our lives in seeking what we consider desirable and avoiding what we consider undesirable.

The Buddha put it this way:

Here one sees a visual object; if it is pleasant, one is attracted; if it is unpleasant, one is repelled. Similarly with sounds, smells, tastes, bodily contacts and mental objects [i.e. thoughts, volitions, emotions, etc.]: if they are pleasant, one is attracted, if they are unpleasant, one is repelled. . . . One who lives thus swayed by likes and dislikes, whenever he experiences a sensation[12] – pleasant, unpleasant or neutral – he reacts by welcoming and enjoying the pleasure, and grows attached to it . . . and so the desire for enjoyment arises in him. And desire for enjoyment causes clinging.[13]

But, as noted above, the ephemeral nature of everything around us is only too obvious. And it is equally obvious that to cling to something that is irremediably transient, and to persist in wanting its preservation, is simply asking for trouble.

The Buddha, working always on the basis of personal experience, not on theory or tradition, taught that the only thing that can actually be said to *exist* is the flow of countless mutually conditioning processes.[14]

What we call the world, material objects, the soul, life itself, is a complex web of transient, ever-changing phenomena, entirely devoid of any lasting essence or permanent identity. This is why the Buddha said that the three basic characteristics of existence are impermanence (*anicca*), not-self or absence of any permanent self-entity (*anattā*), and suffering (*dukkha*). The latter is the corollary of the other two; as long as in our ignorance (*avijjā*) of the impermanent nature of things we persist in clinging to them, frustration is inevitable. It is like pouring water into a sieve and expecting it to stay there. The incorrect perception of what is impermanent as permanent is the root of clinging; we cling because we want. *What* we want is immaterial; whether we want to obtain or to keep something we like, or to avoid something we fear, or to reject something we dislike – it is all wanting. Literally, *we suffer because we want*.

3.3 *The Cessation of Suffering* (dukkha nirodha)

Now, if we suffer because we want, it is obvious that *if we do not want we shall not suffer*. Of course, this is much more easily said than done. Simply to make a resolution 'I do not want to suffer' is worse than useless. In fact, such an attitude is a glaring example of the very desire and attachment that one should try to do away with, since it is simply an expression of the *desire* not to suffer and of *attachment* to comfort and happiness.

This is why the Buddha said: 'The complete fading away and extinction of craving, forsaking it and giving it up, the liberation and detachment from it: this is called the Noble Truth of the Cessation of Suffering.'[15] In saying this he emphasized the need to uproot craving and desire completely, to ensure that it stops and vanishes altogether. But this involves a complete change in our mental attitude. The question is, how can such a change be brought about? And the answer is, again, very simply stated, although, again, far from easy to carry out. It is to cultivate the mindful, non-reactive observation of bodily and mental processes so as to develop an increasingly thorough awareness (undistorted by our usual desires, fears, views, etc.) of their true nature: impermanent, without self and, therefore, involving suffering on our part until we learn to let go.[16] It is through mindful observation of what is actually there that the delusion which makes us perceive that which is impermanent and transient as permanent and lasting is gradually dispelled. Liberation consists in experiencing and understanding fully and clearly that everything is impermanent, and seeing that there is, quite literally, *nothing* to worry about.

This *mindful observation* is meditation. But, of course, it is no good just to sit down somewhere and say to oneself out of the blue, 'Now I am going to meditate', without training or preparation. For one thing, meditation requires a certain skill in using our mental capacities in a specific way and, like all other skills, has to be learned. Secondly, and even more importantly, meditation is an integral part of a whole way of life and, unless it is developed as part of such a way of life, it will not bring about the experience of enlightenment and liberation but will remain at best a mere game or a form of escapism, and at worst may become a dangerous aberration of the powers of the mind. Hence the Buddha's fourth truth, in which he spelled out the appropriate way of life.

3.4 *The Way Leading to the Cessation of Suffering* (dukkha nirodha gāminī paṭipadā)

The analysis of the problem and what causes it is now followed, in this fourth and last truth, by the remedy: a way of life purified by a reasonable moral discipline (*sīla*) and devoted to the achievement of wisdom (*paññā*) through the methodical cultivation of mental concentration (*samādhi*)[17] applied to mindful observation, that is to say, the practice of meditation.

It cannot be sufficiently emphasized that all three components are

17

equally essential. If there is no moral discipline, that is to say, if one does not strive to maintain the purity of one's behaviour, speech and thought, there can be no progress in the cultivation of the mind. And without that mental culture, which is the practice of meditation, there can be no achieving the living wisdom which permeates and transforms the practitioner's experience and behaviour, but only, at the most, a purely intellectual understanding which – although it may be quite subtle and penetrating – cannot transform the deeper levels of the human psyche, which is precisely what needs to be done.

As regards the need for moral discipline, the Buddha's injunctions exemplify the sober approach which is his distinguishing characteristic. The Buddha's way is the Middle Way, which avoids excess and exaggeration and requires good sense and moderation in everything. Certainly, there must be discipline and self-control, but there is no question of excessive asceticism or self-mortification:

To indulge in sensual pleasure is base, common, vulgar, ignoble and unprofitable; to indulge in self-mortification is painful, ignoble and unprofitable. Both these extremes are avoided in the Middle Way, fully realized by the Perfect One, the Way which makes it possible to see and to understand, which leads to peace, to wisdom, to enlightenment, to *nibbāna*.[18]

The Buddha's Middle Way is the way of balance and moderation. For practical purposes, it is expounded in the Buddha's famous formula of the Noble Eightfold Path, so called because it is subdivided into eight factors:

1. *Right View* – that is to say, forming a right opinion of things and achieving a correct understanding.

2. *Right Purpose* – often also called 'Right Thought', i.e. the right kind of intention, based on a correct understanding of the situation.

These two constitute *Wisdom*.

3. *Right Speech* – to abstain from lying, malicious gossip, insulting language, etc.

4. *Right Action* – abstaining from doing things which are harmful to others or to oneself.

5. *Right Livelihood* – not to earn one's living with immoral or illegal activities.

These three make up *Virtue*, or Morality.

6. *Right Effort* – perseverance and energy in cultivating mindfulness and concentration.

7. *Right Mindfulness* – the mindful, unbiased observation of all phenomena in order to perceive them and experience them as they are in actual fact, without emotional or intellectual distortions.

8. *Right Concentration* – the mental concentration essential to calm the mind and sharpen perception.

These three constitute *Meditative Concentration*.

It must be clearly understood that, although the eight factors of the path are enumerated one after the other for purposes of explanation, the idea is not that they should be cultivated successively (i.e. the first one being perfected before going on to the second one, and so on). As was pointed out before, the three main sections of the Path – Morality, Concentration and Wisdom – are indissolubly linked together and operate simultaneously. Wisdom cannot be achieved without meditation, but meditation is ineffective (or sometimes downright harmful) if it does not go together with moral discipline. In fact, they are simply three aspects of the same thing: for an Enlightened One, action, meditation and wisdom are all one and the same – different modes of an integrated, conflict-free consciousness.

At the same time, however, one has to begin somewhere and for this purpose the order in which the eight factors are presented reflects the process normally undergone by someone who undertakes this arduous but supremely rewarding task. One begins by gaining some intellectual understanding of the true nature of the human condition (this is the first stirring of Right Understanding or Right View, the first Path factor). One then decides to do something about it (Right Purpose or Right Thought); this is the beginning of wisdom. One then proceeds to put into practice this new, and still very rudimentary, understanding and resolution in one's behaviour and way of living (Morality, factors 3, 4 and 5) and at the same time devotes time and effort to developing the mental concentration required for mindful observation, which is the practice of meditation (factors 6, 7 and 8).

Progress takes place through the mutual interaction of all factors: meditation, correctly practised, improves understanding or wisdom – one grows increasingly aware of the impermanent and impersonal nature of everything. This greater awareness has, quite naturally, beneficial effects on one's behaviour. In its turn, the greater purity of behaviour in whatever one does, says and thinks provides a better foundation for meditation. Thus a rising spiral is established in which morality, meditation and wisdom grow ever more complete and better integrated, until the full integration of enlightenment is achieved.

Since the present study is intended to focus on the meditative aspect, we shall not have much more to say about the other two sections of the Path in the following pages, but to avoid misunderstandings it is important never to lose sight of the point that has just been made: meditation is not something that happens, or that one does, in a watertight compartment in brief periods specially set aside for the purpose, but it is an integral part of a whole way of life and loses its meaning if cut out of its proper context.

3
The Two Branches of Buddhist Meditation: Samatha and Vipassanā – Tranquillity and Insight

1 In the Buddha's teaching meditation is presented in characteristically sober and pragmatic terms, avoiding all highflown rhetoric. Meditation is described simply as *bhāvanā*, which means 'cultivation' or 'development', terms which – at the same time – accurately define its purpose: to cultivate and develop the vast potential of the mind in order to overcome the unsatisfactory nature of the internal and external circumstances in which we find ourselves. In this context, it must be clearly understood that the Pali term *citta*, which is translated as 'mind', denotes not only the whole area of conscious awareness but embraces also what in modern Western psychological terminology would be referred to as the subconscious and unconscious levels of the human psyche.

As was pointed out before, the unsatisfactoriness of existence is the consequence of unrealistic expectations based on an incorrect perception of the true nature of things. The cultivation and development of the mind is the means whereby this erroneous perception is corrected, and its practice comprises two distinct types of techniques, known respectively as *samatha* and *vipassanā*.

2 *Samatha* means 'tranquillity', 'calm' or 'serenity'. *Samatha* meditation, or tranquillity meditation, aims to achieve states of consciousness characterized by increasingly higher levels of mental tranquillity and stillness. It comprises two elements – the achievement of the highest possible degree of mental concentration and, along with it, the progressive calming of all mental processes. This is achieved through an increasingly concentrated focusing of attention, in which the mind withdraws more and more from all physical and mental stimuli. In this manner there

is a progressive calming of the meditator's mental processes. Highly rarefied states of pure, undistracted consciousness can thus be achieved which are at the same time experiences of a supremely peaceful nature.

The procedure begins by concentrating the mind on certain specific subjects which can be physical or mental (as will be seen in the next chapter), and going systematically through a series of states of mental absorption (*jhāna*). These, which will be described in chapter 5, entail a progressive cutting off of sensory inputs and an increasingly complete suspension of the mind's verbal, rational mode. In the process the meditator attains, for the duration of the exercises, very highly integrated states of consciousness.

This type of Buddhist meditation – which can conveniently be described as *abstractive meditation* because it works through the progressive discarding of sensory and mental stimuli – is, as will readily be seen, very comparable to the meditative techniques used in other traditions. It provides access to states of consciousness characterized by experiences of a holistic nature, which have, of course, great intrinsic value. These experiences, however, are subject to the same law of impermanence as all other things, and their validity is essentially limited to the duration of the state of absorption achieved. This does not, of course, mean that *samatha* meditation is an activity which happens in an entirely closed circuit, with no significant impact on the meditator's everyday life. On the contrary, it is obvious that experiences of this order, in which extremely comprehensive states of bliss, tranquillity and meaningfulness are achieved, cannot but have a generally positive influence on the meditator's mentality, with correspondingly beneficial effects on his everyday behaviour, attitudes and states of mind.

What the absorptions of *samatha* meditation, however, cannot produce is that *permanent* transcendence of the ingrained patterns of the human psyche which is the only condition that can properly be called enlightenment (*bodhi*) – the achievement of the freedom of *nibbāna*. This was the crucial insight in the Buddha's teaching and has often been blurred in later times in spite of the precision with which he formulated it.

Adopting the terminology of modern Western psychologists who are currently studying these aspects of human experience,[19] one can say that *samatha* meditation produces 'altered states of consciousness',[20] which vary in intensity and duration but do not change the fundamental character – the distinctive qualities and characteristics – of consciousness. That is to say, the states of absorption do not produce what one of the leading Western researchers in this field, Daniel Goleman, has called the 'kind of transmutation of awareness [which] is an altered *trait* of consciousness, an enduring change transforming the meditator's every moment'.[21] To obtain this 'enduring change', which is precisely what is traditionally recognized as enlightenment or liberation, it is necessary to turn to *vipassanā*, the characteristically Buddhist type of meditation.

3 *Vipassanā* means literally 'clear vision' (from the verb *vipassati*, to see clearly), to see things precisely as they actually are. The English term 'insight' provides a suitable rendering of the idea, and in fact 'insight meditation' has become, in recent years, the established term for this type of meditation.

Vipassanā, or insight meditation, also begins with concentration exercises, just like *samatha*, using the appropriate meditation subjects. The difference lies in the fact that, in *vipassanā*, one does not go on to ever higher degrees of concentration and absorption. Here, once sufficient concentration has been achieved to ensure that undistracted mindfulness can be maintained (the degree known as 'access concentration', *upacāra samādhi*, or 'momentary concentration', *khaṇika samādhi*), the meditator proceeds to examine with steady, careful attention and in the utmost possible detail precisely all those sensory and mental processes which are discarded in abstractive meditation, including those that normally occur at subconscious or unconscious levels. The purpose here is to achieve complete, direct and immediate awareness of all phenomena, which reveals their basic impermanence (*anicca*) and impersonality (*anattā*), that is to say, the absence of any lasting essence or self-entity in them.[22] It is a matter of achieving full and clear perception of the radical impermanence of all existing phenomena. This includes realizing that what we normally call the 'experiencer' is as impermanent and impersonal, and in exactly the same way, as the object experienced or the experiential process itself. It is this realization, not just accepted as an intellectual postulate but actually lived out in the practice of meditation, which constitutes the insight of *vipassanā*.

4 These are – briefly outlined by way of introduction – the two branches of Buddhist meditation. In the old tradition, meditators would normally practise both: *samatha* in order to develop a high degree of concentration and tranquillity, and *vipassanā* in order to achieve liberation through insight. This combined approach offers clear advantages, since it is obvious that the greater the ability of a meditator to concentrate, and the calmer and more balanced his mental state, the more easily and swiftly he will be able to develop insight.

However, it is very important to bear in mind that tranquillity meditation (*samatha*) cannot by itself, as has already been pointed out, produce enlightenment. This can only be achieved through the development of insight (*vipassanā*), which can be adequately practised on the basis of a reasonable minimum level of concentration (access or momentary concentration), without the need for going through the various stages of absorption (*jhāna*).

It is also worth noting that the absorptions may entail their own kind of risk in that – precisely because of the achievement of temporary but highly rewarding altered states of consciousness – the meditator may come to consider the absorptions as ends in themselves, in which case they will hinder rather than help the progress of insight.

It is for this reason that, depending on character and circumstances, certain meditators soon started practising pure insight (*sukkha vipassanā*), i.e. pursuing the development of insight without the parallel development of the advanced stages of tranquillity. Increasing numbers of meditators have been turning to the practice of pure insight in recent times. This is not surprising in view of the stresses and constraints of modern life, which make it more difficult than in the past to find both the time and the appropriate environment to practise tranquillity meditation, which generally requires rather more leisure and seclusion. This is especially true in the case of meditators who are neither monks nor recluses, but who, like many people today in the West as in the East, are trying to combine the practice of meditation with the multiple personal, social and professional demands of a layman's life.

5 The fact that both types of meditation – tranquillity and insight – begin with the same kinds of concentration exercises, as well as the similarity between the tranquillity meditation of Buddhism and the meditative practices of other traditions, have been the cause of many confusions and misunderstandings (even among supposedly knowledgeable students of the subject) concerning the true nature of Buddhist meditation and its distinguishing characteristics. This is why it may not be superfluous, even at the cost of some repetition, to recapitulate the essential features of the two branches of Buddhist meditation – tranquillity and insight – before going into the details of the two techniques in the following chapters.

What the two types of meditation have in common is that they are both *attention-training methods*.[23] The basic difference between the two lies in their aims and, beyond a certain point, in their methods. *Samatha* (abstractive tranquillity meditation) pursues the utmost degree of mental concentration, progressively discarding all the sensory and mental inputs which normally occupy the mind, to concentrate exclusively on the single percept, image or idea selected as the subject of meditation. It is rather like bringing down a light beam to the sharpest possible focus on one single, intensely bright point. The high levels of mental concentration and absorption thus achieved represent altered states of consciousness,[24] which have well-defined differential characteristics, such as a suspension of sense perception, interruption of the verbal, rational activities of the mind, and feelings of bliss, happiness, serenity and ineffable intuition. These states of consciousness are clearly distinct from the three main states of ordinary consciousness, as defined in psychology, namely waking, sleeping and dreaming, and they are incompatible with them. When you are in one of the states of absorption (*jhāna*) you are neither awake, nor asleep, nor dreaming; you are operating in a specifically distinct mode.

In *vipassanā* (insight meditation), on the other hand, mental concentration is cultivated only up to the degree which is sufficient to ensure a steady, undistracted mindfulness. The resulting alert and receptive state of mind is then used to develop an uninterrupted and finely perceptive awareness of whatever comes up before consciousness (whether from internal or external sources), involving the full, continuous and fully conscious exercise of all mental faculties. In terms of the previous comparison, we could say that here the beam of light is not narrowed down to an infinitesimal point, but only to a size which will provide a powerful and finely focused but rather broader light field, which follows and illuminates whatever is happening at any given moment. This exercise, assiduously practised and refined, becomes an increasingly intense and characteristic manner of experiencing, which is not a state of consciousness intrinsically different from the ordinary states, but is a modification which opens them up to a new dimension. One is then operating not outside the ordinary states of consciousness, but within them in a new way. Their normal functions remain fully available (working, in fact, more efficiently) and, in addition, some new functions of positive value emerge that are not otherwise present in them. This is best described as a thoroughgoing reorganization of the human psyche. The person who experiences the insight of *vipassanā* lives differently, whether waking, dreaming or even sleeping. The new manner is distinguished by, among others, a sense of detachment, psychological and mental balance, openness and availability to others, and exceptional relevance and functionality of thought and action. This is what one of the most authoritative exponents of the modern school of transpersonal psychology has defined as a *higher state of consciousness*.[25] It is a true transmutation which produces new, indelible traits of consciousness. This transmutation is what is traditionally called enlightenment or liberation and, in its highest degree, *nibbāna*.[26]

A word of warning: do not expect instant enlightenment; this transmutation is not something that happens all at once, but rather in progressive stages (even though the transition from one stage to the next is, in itself, the sudden culmination of a prior process). This is a gradual restructuring of the human psyche, demanding much time and perseverance, which is hardly surprising considering how much there is that needs improving and reshaping in most of us.

4
Concentration, the Basis for Meditation

1 The Three Levels of Concentration

Before discussing tranquillity and insight meditation individually, it is necessary to consider the basic element they have in common – mental concentration – and how it is developed.

For the purpose of meditative practice, three different levels, or degrees of intensity, of concentration may be distinguished.

1.1 Preparatory Concentration (parikamma samādhi)

This is simply the initial effort that one makes to concentrate when beginning the mental exercise. It is the kind of concentration one normally exercises in daily life when paying conscious attention to a specific object. Naturally, the degree of attentiveness varies depending on each person's natural – untrained – ability to concentrate, and in this there are very considerable differences. Some people concentrate quite easily and powerfully, while others have difficulty in keeping their minds on any one thing for any length of time. However, even in the case of someone who concentrates easily but who has not specially trained to do so, this preparatory concentration is not sufficient to practise meditation. It is therefore necessary to stabilize and strengthen it, and this is done by focusing on an appropriate 'meditation subject' (such as described later in this chapter), until the attainment of access concentration.

1.2 Access Concentration (upacāra samādhi)

This is so called because it gives access both to the practice of tranquillity and of insight. When used for insight meditation it is traditionally referred to as 'momentary concentration' (*khaṇika samādhi*). The distinguishing characteristic of this level is a steady and intense concentration of mental attention on the meditation subject, taken either in its original form or (in certain categories of exercises) in the form of the so-called 'counterpart sign', as will be seen later.[27] At this stage there is no inhibition as yet in the reception of sensory and mental inputs. The meditator is fully aware of what is happening both within and around him, but *it no longer distracts him*. His attention remains centred on the meditation subject.

From here on the two types of meditation go their separate ways. For the purposes of insight (*vipassanā*), this level of access (or momentary) concentration is enough to practise the mindful observation of all phenomena and processes, and thus develop an ever finer and more complete, direct awareness of their transient, unstable nature. For the pursuit of tranquillity (*samatha*), on the other hand, it is necessary to continue strengthening and refining the concentration of the mind, in order to achieve fixed concentration.

1.3 *Fixed Concentration (*appanā samādhi*) – The Concentration of attainment*

Here the mind becomes fully absorbed in the meditation subject (or its counterpart sign) to the exclusion of all other thoughts or percepts. This is *fixed concentration*, also known as *attainment concentration* because it is through this that the various levels of meditative absorption (*jhāna*) are attained. As the meditator deepens and refines this mental state (moving up through successive absorptions), he lives through experiences of an increasingly unitive, or holistic, character. The experiential factors of multiplicity and diversity are progressively replaced by a flow of pure consciousness, in which there is a melting away of any distinction between the observer, what is observed and the process of observation.

2 *Concentration Exercises: Perceptual and Reflective*

Basically, there are two ways of practising mental concentration, which may be broadly distinguished as *perceptual* and *reflective*, depending on the mental functions involved.

2.1 In the case of *perceptual* exercises attention is directed entirely to the bare perception of the object or process selected as the meditation subject, exactly as it is found at any given moment, without going into any kind of reflection, reasoning or imagining about it. The immediate, direct perception, moment by moment, of the meditation subject, excluding all distractions, whether sensory (other percepts), intellectual (pursuing trains of thought about the object or started off by it) or emotional (dwelling on any emotional connotations) fixes the mind on each specific moment of perception as it occurs. This fixing of the mind on the infinitesimal here-and-now is what the old texts call the 'unification of the mind'.[28]

For this type of practice, any kind of sensory input may be selected (e.g. visual objects, sounds, touch sensations, even smells or tastes). However, since it is clearly desirable to work with a sensory input which is as steady and continuous as possible, traditional Buddhist meditation gives preference to the senses of sight (perception of colours, shapes, etc.) and touch (sensations in the meditator's own body). In certain exercises use is also made of what may be called indirect or derived visual perception. This consists in the detailed mental visualization of objects which are not available for direct visual inspection, either because they are not normally visible (such as, for instance, the internal organs in the exercise consisting in the contemplation of the parts of the body[29]), or because they are no longer available at the time of the exercise (such as the contemplation of the progressive stages of body decay after death[30]). These visualizations are based on circumstantial descriptions which have been memorized beforehand and, where possible, on earlier inspection of the objects when available (as in the case of bodies seen on charnel grounds).

2.2 *Reflective* exercises, on the other hand, leave sensory perception aside, using purely mental materials as meditation subjects. In typical exercises of this kind, the meditator begins by reflecting on the nature and significance of certain entities (such as the Buddha, the *Dhamma*, etc.) or fundamental truths (impermanence, death). Here it is the sustained application of the mind, with deliberate exclusion of distracting inputs (such as sense data or the constant haze of extraneous mental activity which usually surrounds our 'normal' thinking), which brings about the increasing concentration of the mind.

3 The Three Signs of Concentration

In the case of perceptual exercises, the first two levels of concentration – that is, preparatory concentration and access (or momentary) concentration – are correlated with three 'signs' (*nimitta*). These are distinctive perceptual experiences which mark the progress of mental concentration.

3.1 *The Preliminary Sign* (parikamma nimitta)

This is simply the initial, normal sense perception of the meditation subject as one begins to focus one's attention consciously and exclusively on it.

3.2 *The Learning Sign* (uggaha nimitta)

As the focus of attention grows steadier and more intense, the meditator develops a continuous and detailed perception of the subject, which remains clear even in the intervals when there is no direct observation (for instance, when closing one's eyes for a few moments during the contemplation of a visual subject). This continuity of the image at the neural level is what is called the 'learning sign' or sometimes also, for obvious reasons, the 'acquired image'. It is an indication of the fact that the mind is beginning to hold on to the perception of the subject in an assured, undistracted manner.

It is worth quoting the traditional description of this condition. For this purpose, the best source is the *Visuddhi Magga* (*The Path of Purification*), a classic of Buddhist literature composed in Sri Lanka by the Monk Buddhaghosa in the fifth century BC. This is a comprehensive and minutely detailed handbook of Buddhist meditation, based on the Buddha's *Discourses* and the early commentaries, which has served as an invaluable guide to practitioners down the centuries. I shall often have occasion to refer to it from now on when discussing specific aspects of meditative practice. According to this manual, when concentrating on a visual subject,

> it should be adverted to now with eyes open, now with eyes shut. And he [the meditator] should go on developing it in this way a hundred times, a thousand times, and even more than that, until the learning sign arises. When, while he is developing it in this way, it comes into focus as he adverts with his eyes shut exactly as it does with his eyes open, then the learning sign it said to have been produced.[31]

3.3 *The Counterpart Sign* (patibhāga nimitta)

As the meditator goes on practising with the learning sign as a base, he eventually reaches a higher degree of concentration – *access concentration* – as indicated by the appearance of the *counterpart sign*. This is no longer the direct image of the initial subject but a percept with its own characteristics, which vary, as will be seen, depending on the nature of the original subject, but which are no longer in any way representational of it. The counterpart sign is an experience in its own right which, essentially, indicates the coming into awareness of the perceptual act itself – the conscious perception of perception. It is described as follows in the *Visuddhi Magga*:

The difference between the earlier learning sign and the counterpart sign is this. In the learning sign any fault in the *kasiṇa*[32] is apparent [i.e. any irregularity in the visual object taken as meditation subject; the acquired image one 'sees' with one's eyes closed, being an exact representation, naturally shows the same characteristic features of the original material object]. But the counterpart sign appears as if it were breaking out from the learning sign, and a hundred times, a thousand times, more purified, like a looking-glass disc drawn from its case, like a mother-of-pearl dish well washed, like the moon's disc coming out from behind a cloud, like cranes against a thunder cloud. But it has neither colour nor shape; for if it had, it would be cognizable by the eye, gross, susceptible of comprehension and stamped with the three characteristics[33] [i.e. it would be a material thing that could be known as such]. But it is not like that. For it is born only of perception in one who has obtained concentration, being a mere mode of appearance.[34]

It will be appreciated that at this point we are moving into an area of experience which is difficult to describe adequately and without being misleading. This is one of the reasons why meditation masters normally refrain from explaining or describing to their students in advance the kinds of experiences that may result. The other, and more important, reason for such caution is that a prior description is more likely to hinder than to help progress by generating expectations. In fact, if the student is hoping and wishing for a certain sensation or experience which he has been told is a sign of progress, he runs a double risk. First, his thinking about 'getting the sign' may interfere with his concentration, which is the only way of actually developing the sign. Secondly, and more dangerously, the student may start imagining the sign along the lines of the description that has been furnished to him and may, through a process of auto-suggestion, convince himself that he is perceiving it, when all he is doing is indulging in wilful constructs of the imagination – which is precisely the opposite of true concentration.

To make progress the meditator must hold fast to one thing only: the absolute need to keep his attention steady on the meditation subject. The signs, when they occur, will do so unbidden, of their own accord, as correlates of the degree of concentration achieved. In addition, it must be borne in mind that this correlation is not a mathematical kind of correspondence, with strictly defined ratios between degree of concentration and clarity or intensity of the sign. As is always the case when you are dealing with living realities rather than theoretical abstractions, there is a very wide margin of individual variation. Depending on the person, his capabilities and the circumstances of the case, the development of the signs may be easy or difficult, swift or long-delayed, intense or weak, and there are even people who achieve access concentration with barely perceptible learning and counterpart signs.

4 Meditation Subjects

Broadly speaking, almost any physical or mental data may be used as a subject on which to concentrate one's attention. Experience, however, has shown that certain kinds of subjects, because of their own inherent characteristics, are more favourable than others for the beginning and further development of mental concentration. To take for instance visual subjects, it can readily be appreciated that it is better if they are simple and homogeneous in appearance, thus providing less opportunity for the mind – which loves diversity – to start all sorts of thought processes (comparisons, reflections, associations, etc.) which are the primary hindrances to concentration. Some reflective meditation exercises, on the other hand, in which the meditator is invited to reflect, following certain specified patterns, on the nature of, for instance, the Buddha, the *Dhamma*, etc., or on qualities such as loving kindness, compassion or equanimity, are based on fairly complex intellectual activity but can be very beneficial by generating strong motivation. In selecting the meditation subject for each student at any given time the meditation master is guided by two basic considerations: the character and mentality of the student and the type of meditation which is to be practised (tranquillity or insight).

In the old tradition of Buddhist meditation, forty specific meditation subjects are recommended. These are ten *kasinas*,[35] ten kinds of body decay, ten recollections, one perception, one analysis, four sublime states (or divine abidings) and four immaterial states. For the practice of formal meditation sessions with any of these subjects, it is recommended to select a quiet spot free from external distractions and to sit down in a comfortable position. The traditional posture is, of course, crosslegged (either in lotus, half-lotus or simply tailor-fashion), but this is not essential. The important point is to take up a position which can be maintained comfortably without moving for the longest possible time. One exception to this is the so-called 'walking meditation' (*cankamana*) exercise, which, as its name indicates, consists in focusing attention on the movements involved in walking. This is a variant of the contemplation of the body (see 4.3.9.1 below and chapter 6).

4.1 *The Ten* Kasiṇas

These are earth, water, fire, air (the four elements); blue, yellow, red, white (the four basic colours); light, and limited space.

The meditation subjects 'earth', 'water' and 'fire', as well as the four colours, can be contemplated directly from nature by an experienced meditator, by looking, for instance, at a recently ploughed field, a lake or pond, the flames of a fire, and the colours as they appear in nature (flowers, shrubs, etc.). 'Light' and 'limited space' may also be taken as they appear in the frame of an open door or window.

A beginner, on the other hand, will need to construct a *kasiṇa* – a simple display device to be used as an aid in meditation. This should consist of a circular surface (a convenient size is about 1 foot, or 30 cm, in diameter[36]) made entirely of the material or colour required. It is essential that the visible surface should be as uniform as possible. In the case of the colours, a disc of any suitable material (wood, cardboard, etc.) can be covered with the appropriate paint, or else one may fill a tray with objects of the right colour (flowers or a cloth, for instance). If flowers are used, one should ensure that only the coloured petals are visible, without stalks, leaves or twigs, which could distract one's attention from the colour. To make an earth or a water *kasiṇa*, a quantity of either may be placed in a circular container (tray, shallow dish, etc.). In the case of the colours and of 'earth', care should be taken to ensure that the resulting surface is as smooth and even as possible, both in colour and in texture. As for 'fire', this may be observed through a round opening cut in a screen of cloth or other material placed between the meditator and the flames. The 'light' *kasiṇa* may be obtained by projecting a light beam onto a wall or any other smooth surface, and 'limited space' is displayed by cutting a round opening in a wall, partition or any other suitable vertical surface. As far as the contemplation of 'air' is concerned, there is no difference in method between beginners and experienced practitioners. There is no device or artefact, but air should be contemplated either by noticing the movement of plants, trees or shrubs swaying in the breeze, or by focusing on the touch of air on one's skin.

Except in this latter case, for all other *kasiṇas* the beginner, after placing the device in a convenient spot, should sit down on a stool, or a low chair, about 3–4 feet (1 metre) from the device and focus his attention on it. The *Visuddhi Magga*'s instructions in this respect are both picturesque and practical:

> He should seat himself on a well-covered chair, with legs a span and four fingers high, prepared in a place that is two and a half cubits [that is, two and a half times the distance from elbow to fingertip] from the kasiṇa disk. The kasiṇa does not appear plainly to him if he sits further off than that, and if he sits nearer faults in the kasiṇa appear. If he sits higher up, he has to look at it with his neck bent, and if he sits lower down, his knees ache.[37]

These are all purely perceptual exercises, and the mind should be concentrated exclusively on the perception of the selected subject without starting or pursuing any trains of thought or mental associations related to it. Moreover, the perception itself must concentrate increasingly on the essential aspect of the subject, leaving aside any accidental or subsidiary elements. For instance, when contemplating the colour 'blue', one begins with the kasiṇa as it is, noting whatever irregularities in colour or texture may be present (e.g. uneven distribution of the paint in the case of a painted disc, wrinkles or folds in the cloth, or remains of leaves or stems if flowers are used). Then the irregularities should be ignored and the mind concentrated as powerfully as possible on the pure blue colour. At the beginning it often helps to repeat mentally, at the same time, the word 'blue, blue' until a good perception has been established. Or, in the case of the earth kasiṇa, the colour of the earth should be ignored, as well as any unevenness of the surface, and there should be only the thought and perception of 'earth, earth'.

These ten kasiṇa exercises, being of the perceptual type, have their corresponding learning and counterpart signs. Briefly, according to the *Visuddhi Magga*, these are as follows:

The Four Colours

The signs are the same for all the four colours – blue, yellow, red and white. In the learning sign, 'any fault in the kasiṇa is evident . . . ; the stamens and stalks [when flowers are used] and the gaps between the petals, etc., are apparent. The counterpart sign appears like a crystal fan in space,[38] free from the kasiṇa disc.[39]

Earth

Here too, 'in the learning sign any fault in the kasiṇa is apparent'[40] (any irregularities in the colour or texture of the earth with which the container has been filled), while the counterpart sign has its own characteristics, which we have already quoted as an example when discussing the counterpart sign in general (section 3.3 above), and which are formulated in terms of brightness, clarity and purity (mirror, mother-of-pearl, moon, etc.).

Water

The learning sign has the appearance of moving. If the water has bubbles of froth mixed with it, the learning sign has the same appearance, and it is evident as a fault in the *kasina*. But the counterpart sign appears inactive, like a crystal fan set in space, like the disc of a looking glass made of crystal.[41]

Fire

Herein, the learning sign appears like a sinking down, as the flame keeps detaching itself. But when someone apprehends it in a *kasina* that is not made up,[42] any fault in the *kasina* is evident [in the learning sign], and any firebrand, or pile of embers or ashes, or smoke appears in it. The counterpart sign appears motionless like a piece of red cloth set in space, like a gold fan, like a gold column.[43]

Air

Here the learning sign appears to move like the swirl of hot [steam] on rice gruel just withdrawn from an oven. The counterpart sign is quiet and motionless.[44]

Light

Here the learning sign is like the circle [of light] thrown on the wall or the ground. The counterpart sign is like a compact bright cluster of lights.[45]

Limited Space

Here the learning sign resembles the hole together with the wall, etc., that surrounds it. . . . The counterpart sign appears only as a circle of space.[46]

4.2 *The Ten Kinds of Body Decay*

These are also perceptual exercises (and correspond to the 'cemetery contemplations' which are one of the forms of 'contemplation of the body', as will be seen in section 4.3.9 below). Here the meditator contemplates dead bodies in different stages of decay – bloated, livid, festering, dismembered, scattered bones, etc. The exercises begin with the direct inspection of a corpse, and continue with detailed mental visualizations, which must keep vividly present in the mind, in all its details, the condition of decay which has been physically perceived to begin with.

The prerequisite for these exercises is therefore the availability of a corpse. This was not at all difficult to find in ancient India (where the dead were normally not buried or burned, but placed in the charnel grounds outside the villages, there to decay or be devoured by scavengers), but is rather less easy today, especially in Western countries. Moreover, strict supervision by a qualified teacher is even more essential in these exercises than in others, because of the more immediate psychological and emotional repercussions which they may have. In spite of the fact, therefore, that this category of meditation subjects is very useful in correcting excessive attachment to the appearance and wellbeing of one's own body, and to sensual pleasures in general, there is little point in discussing them in detail in a book such as this.

4.3 *The Ten Recollections*

With two important exceptions these are meditations of the reflective kind and differ in this respect from the ones we have been considering so far. In these reflective exercises, sometimes also called recollections, the starting point is, in each case, a traditional form of words which summarizes the essential points or characteristics of the meditation subject, to be reviewed in the course of the recollective exercise. The meditator begins by mentally reciting the appropriate formula and then concentrates his attention successively on each one of the elements of which it is composed, reflecting carefully upon it. One begins generally by considering the semantic aspect – the meaning and connotations of the words – moving on subsequently to their deeper significance as an expression, manifestation or sign of the truths explained and demonstrated by the Buddha. This reflective concentration sharpens the awareness of these liberating truths, and the progressive strengthening and focusing of awareness, in its turn, strengthens concentration. Let us briefly consider the eight reflective meditations, with their traditional formulations. First of all, there are the so-called 'Three Jewels' (*ti-ratana*), which are at the same time the 'Three Refuges' (*ti-saraṇa*) of the Buddhist: the *Buddha* (the Enlightened One), the *Dhamma* (the Teaching) and the *Sangha* (the Community).

4.3.1 *The Buddha*

Formula
Such, indeed, is that Blessed One, worthy, fully enlightened, endowed with knowledge and virtue, well-gone, knower of worlds, incomparable leader of men to be tamed, teacher of gods and men, enlightened and blessed.[47]

Meditation
The meditator now takes up each one of the elements of the formula – Blessed One, worthy, fully enlightened, etc. – and reflects on them in the manner just outlined. The *Visuddhi Magga* offers detailed instruction

on how to reflect on each one of the terms of the formula, including a great variety of alternatives. These cannot, of course, be gone into here, but just by way of illustration, here are a few of the ways in which the first term of the recollection of the Buddha may be reflected upon. One may begin by considering that 'Blessed' is a term signifying the respect and veneration accorded to the Buddha as the highest of all beings and distinguished by his special qualities. One may then go on to reflect on these qualities in various ways; for instance, the Buddha is 'blessed' in what he attains, in what he abolishes, in what he possesses and in what he understands, that is to say, he attains the supreme achievement of virtue, universal love, compassion, equanimity, etc., and the supreme blessedness of *nibbāna*; he entirely abolishes greed, hate and delusion, as well as any blemishes or shortcomings in mindfulness and awareness, and all anger, ill will, conceit, etc.; he possesses full control of the mind, full realization of truth, perfection and the fruit of pure endeavour, etc.; he understands and teaches the Four Noble Truths: suffering, its origin in clinging due to ignorance, its cessation through the elimination of ignorance, and the path that leads to the cessation of suffering. In this and similar ways the meditator reflects deeply and repeatedly on each of the terms that make up the formula.

4.3.2 *The* Dhamma

Formula
The Teaching (*Dhamma*) is well proclaimed by the Blessed One, visible here and now, with immediate fruit, inviting investigation, onward-leading, and directly experienceable by the wise.[48]

Meditation
'Well proclaimed' because it announces and describes the way of life that leads to enlightenment, and because it is good in the beginning, the middle, and the end. It is good in the beginning because it starts by promoting virtue and, with it, one's own physical and mental wellbeing; it is good in the middle (i.e. as one progresses in the practice of the Teaching) as producing tranquillity (*samatha*) and insight (*vipassanā*); it is good in the end with the achievement of *nibbāna*. 'Visible here and now' – the Teaching is visible here and now because anyone who practises it properly and does away with craving, clinging, etc., soon perceives its benefits in and by himself, without having to place blind faith in what someone else claims for it. And so on, with each one of the other terms.

4.3.3 *The Sangha*

Formula
The Community (*Sangha*) of the Blessed One's disciples is the one which has entered on the good way, on the straight way, on the true way, on the proper way, that is to say, the four pairs of persons, the eight kinds of individuals;[49] this Community of the Blessed One's disciples is worthy of gifts, worthy of hospitality, worthy of offerings, worthy of reverence, as an incomparable field of merit[50] for the world.[51]

Meditation
'The Community of the Blessed One's disciples': the disciples are those who hear attentively the Blessed One's instruction and are guided by it. All of them together form a communality because they possess in common the *right view* of things and the *right purpose* in dealing with them (the first two factors of the Noble Path), as well as the practice of virtue (factors three to five of the Noble Path, i.e. *right speech, action* and *livelihood*); in addition, by engaging in meditation they practise the sixth, seventh and eighth factors of the Path (*right effort, mindfulness* and *concentration*), so that they practise the Eightfold Noble Path in its entirety. This is why it is said that they have 'entered on the good way' – the way regulated by the Teaching – which leads 'straight' to liberation, which is 'true' and 'proper' because it embodies the correct pursuit of the truth of *nibbāna*, etc.

The next three recollections on the traditional list concern various aspects of virtue. The first one of these three refers to the general practice of virtuous living, i.e. the moral discipline of thought, speech and action which represents virtue, or morality, as one of the three main subdivisions of the Path (as shown in chapter 2, section 3.4).

4.3.4 *Virtue*

Formula
The recollection should concentrate on the various kinds of virtues to be practised, which are 'untorn, unrent, unblotched and unmottled, liberating, praised by the wise, not adhered to, and conducive to concentration.'[52]

Meditation
The point here is to develop the fullest possible awareness of the importance of leading a scrupulously virtuous life, without equivocation or

compromise, and to promote the sense of integrity inherent in such living as a powerful means of developing mental concentration. As in the previous exercises in this group, 'recollection' takes place by reflecting in detail on the full meaning and connotations of each one of the terms. For instance, virtues are 'untorn and unrent' when one manages to maintain an unbroken, stable continuity of pure and virtuous thought and volition, without breaking it with immoral or improper words, thoughts or actions. Here one contemplates unbroken integrity of virtue. 'Unblotched and unmottled': without any impairment in the intensity and purity, i.e. contemplating the highest degree of the state of virtue. Similarly with the other terms. The reference to 'not adhered to' is important; here the meditator must recollect the need not to become attached to his or her own virtue, to avoid any self-satisfaction or self-righteousness, which are serious contaminations of virtue.

4.3.5 *Generosity*

The second recollection of virtues concentrates on generosity as its subject. Of course, this must go together with the actual practice 'of giving and sharing . . . according to one's means and one's ability' (as the *Visuddhi Magga* does not fail to stress). Recollection – which takes place term by term, in the usual manner – is based on the formula:

It is gain for me, it is great gain for me, that in a generation obsessed by the stain of avarice I abide with my heart free from stain by avarice, and am freely generous and open-handed, that I delight in relinquishing, expect to be asked, and rejoice in giving and sharing.[53]

4.3.6 *Recollection of Deities*

The third recollection of virtues is performed by taking one's own qualities of faith, goodness and so on, developed by means of the Noble Path, and by taking the figures of deities as examples, paragons and witnesses of these virtues. Here, the traditional formula evokes a whole range of divinities who form the pantheon of popular Buddhism in Asia as adapted from Hinduism. This turning to divinities may seem odd in the light of the Buddha's own insistence on the uselessness of metaphysical and theological speculation, to the extent that Buddhism has sometimes been quite properly called 'a religion without a god'. The contradiction, however, is more apparent than real. The main point to bear in mind is that the Buddha did not fail to recognize the reality of orders of existence outside and beyond the material sphere with which we are familiar in everyday life. As we are told, he had, in fact, direct knowledge of such other modes of existence, thanks to the extraordinary development of his faculties, which opened up to him a much broader and subtler range of perception and understanding than the 'normal' one. He was, therefore, aware of the existence of beings operating in ranges outside ordinary human awareness and endowed with powers and faculties different from, and sometimes higher than, those of human beings. More or less obscurely aware of such beings at different times, humankind has variously called them, down the ages, gods, angels, demons, genii, spirits, etc. The Buddha had therefore no difficulty in accepting the popular beliefs of those to whom his teaching was addressed, and even the names and mythologies with which they supplied them, since he well knew that these beliefs reflected a perception – even though a confused and distorted one – of something that actually existed. He always stressed, however, quite firmly – and this is the essential point – that all these beings and powers are no more real or permanent than we ourselves and, although sometimes vastly more lasting when measured in human terms, in no sense eternal. Like all that exists, the gods, too, are subject to the law of *kamma*, to the complex, unbroken interaction of causes and effects. Thus the Buddha taught that 'deities', like all other orders of beings, are equally subject to the consequences of their actions, and that their existence (immensely more privileged, blissful or durable though it may appear than ours), is equally subject to change, dissolution and rebirth, again and again, until and unless *nibbāna* is achieved, which is the only definitive liberation. In Buddhism gods are brothers to men, as men are to beasts. We are all on the same continuum, although at different points. This may briefly help to explain the point of this recollection, which appears at first to be different from the others.

The point of the exercise is definitely *not* to send prayers up to any deities or to beg for their assistance, but to take them as examples of other levels of existence and awareness (still subject to change and transience, even if on different timescales) and especially as witnesses to our efforts to perfect positive qualities in ourselves.

In this case there is little point in reproducing the formula for recollection in its traditional terms since the deities mentioned therein are not familiar to Western readers. Anyone wishing to practise this recollection, however, may simply refer to the divine or spiritual manifestations which may be most meaningful to him, depending on his own religious, cultural and ethnic background. The outline of the formula, which everyone can fill out accordingly, would be something like this:

There are [here think of the relevant deities] . . . , and those deities were possessed of faith[54] . . . , of virtue . . . , of learning . . . , of generosity . . . , of understanding such that when they died here, they were reborn there.[55] And such faith, virtue, learning, generosity and understanding are present in me too.

Meditation

The *Visuddhi Magga* explains that in recollecting these qualities, first in the deities as examples of high achievement and then in himself, the meditator takes the deities as witnesses: 'He should go into solitary retreat and recollect his own special qualities of faith, etc., with deities standing as witnesses.'[56]

4.3.7 Mindfulness of Death

For this recollection, the most universally relevant and, to the unprepared mind, perhaps the most harrowing, the shortest formula consists simply in considering that 'Death will take place; the life faculty will be interrupted' or, even more simply, 'Death, death'. However, for those who do not find these simple considerations sufficient, the *Visuddhi Magga* suggests eight different ways of recollecting death. Each one of these is given complete with one or more formulas, which would take too long to reproduce here. In any case, it is not difficult for everyone to develop appropriate recollections on these eight ways, so that it may suffice to list them briefly.

4.3.7.1 Death as a Murderer

It stalks us as a murderer his victim – it begins moving towards us as we are born and, when it reaches us, it kills us.

4.3.7.2 Death as the Ruin of Success

No achievement is eternal; all greatness and success end, sooner or later, in ruin. All health ends in sickness, all youth in ageing, all life in death.

4.3.7.3 By Comparing Oneself to Others

Since the beginning of time all men have been subject to death, even the most powerful, the strongest, the wisest, the holiest. None have been spared. Even the Buddha himself, 'who was the equal of those without equal, without double, accomplished and fully enlightened, – even he was suddenly quenched by the downpour of death's rain, as a great mass of fire is quenched by the downpour of a rain of water.'[57] Death will come to me just as it did to all those outstanding beings.

This is, of course, the familiar theme of the Dance of Death, ubiquitous in painting and poetry in the European Middle Ages, with the grim Reaper impartially cutting down kings and beggars, warriors and monks, the rich and the poor, the young and the old.

4.3.7.4 *Recollection as to Sharing the Body with Many*

One should clearly realize that the body is a community composed of innumerable individual living cells, constantly decaying and being replaced, and shared by many different bacteria, microbes and other micro-organisms which live and die within us; and also that the organism is constantly exposed to internal and external attacks, such as diseases, accidents, etc., and that this community always falls apart in the end.[58]

4.3.7.5 *The Frailty of Life*

Consider the extent to which not only the wellbeing but the very existence of one's organism depend on just a few factors: air for breathing, food, quite a narrow range of environmental temperatures, the delicate balance of the elements making up the organism. When one of these is disturbed or lacking (in some cases, such as air, even just for a very short time), death ensues.

4.3.7.6 *The Unpredictability of Death*

Recollect that nothing is predictable about death. One does not know when or how it will occur, nor where one's body will be laid down, nor where a future existence will arise.[59] The only thing that is certain beyond doubt is that death will occur.

4.3.7.7 *The Brevity of Life*

One who lives long may live to be a hundred years old, but one may also drop down dead before reading to the bottom of this page. Death is always just round the corner. One should therefore live each moment as if it were the last, with full awareness.

4.3.7.8 *The Shortness of the Moment*

If you think about it carefully, you realize that, properly speaking, the real experience of actual living pertains only to the present moment, to 'now'. Everything else is either already past (even if it was only a moment ago), and belongs thus to the realm of memory, or has not yet happened and belongs to the future realm of expectation, anticipation, hope or fear, etc. But the succession of 'nows' is infinitely swift: by the time you have read the word 'now' it is already in the past – and so is the 'you' who read it. The next 'now' is another moment, with another reader. The present moment is a mere flash, an infinitesimal instant, a matter of less than microseconds. The *Visuddhi Magga* says:

Just as a chariot wheel, when it is rolling, rolls only on one point of its tyre [i.e. touches the ground only with one point of its circumference at any given moment] and, when it is at rest, rests only on one point, so too the life of living beings lasts only for a single conscious moment.[60]

What we call 'life' is the swift unbroken succession of such moments, each one of which has its own distinct and (even if only infinitesimally) different character from the one before and the one after. Each moment of 'life' is a rebirth following upon the death of the preceding one.

4.3.8 Recollection of Peace

The last of the purely reflective, or recollective, meditations concerns the qualities of *nibbāna*, in other words, the stilling of all suffering.

Formula

In so far as there are *dhammas* [phenomena], whether conditioned or unconditioned,[61] fading away[62] is pronounced the best of them, that is to say, the disillusionment of vanity, the elimination of thirst, the abolition of dependence, the termination of the round, the destruction of craving, fading away, cessation, *nibbāna*.[63]

The recollection is practised, as in the other exercises of this group, by considering each one of the terms individually (see also chapter 7 below, on *nibbāna*).

We must now turn to the only two exercises in this group of the ten so-called recollections which are based not on mental reflection but on direct perception. As such, they are extremely important because – by the very fact that they constitute exercises in clarity of perception – they are particularly suited to the development of insight (*vipassanā*) being, in fact, the two exercises most commonly used for this purpose. These are 'mindfulness of the body' and 'mindfulness of breathing' (the latter being, in fact, a special case of the former, since breathing is, of course,

43

one of the most fundamental bodily processes). In chapter 6, which is entirely devoted to *vipassanā*, we shall see how mindfulness of the body, in its various applications, constitutes the first of the four 'foundations of mindfulness' for the development of insight. At this point I shall therefore do no more than briefly identify the variants of mindfulness of the body which can be used to practise concentration.

4.3.9 *Mindfulness of the Body* (kāyagatāsati)

Of all meditation subjects, the perception of one's own body is one of the most important for the practice of Buddhist meditation. In fact, the *Visuddhi Magga* maintains that it is the characteristically Buddhist kind of meditation, stating that it 'is never promulgated except after an Enlightened One's arising,[64] and is outside the province of any sectarians'.[65]

Mindfulness of the body may be practised in different ways, focusing on different aspects. The traditional exercises are as follows.

4.3.9.1 *Mindfulness of the Bodily Postures*

Going, standing, sitting or lying down.

4.3.9.2 *The Four Kinds of Full Awareness (or Clear Comprehension)*

This consists in performing every action – eating, drinking, moving, speaking, keeping silent, fetching and carrying – with full awareness of what is being done, and how, and with a clear understanding of (a) the purpose, (b) the suitability of the means employed, (c) the appropriate sphere of action and (d) the real nature of the situation.

4.3.9.3 *The Body as Composed of the Four Primary Elements*

The body is considered as the composite result of the four primary states or conditions of matter: solid, liquid, gaseous and radiant, which correspond to increasing degrees of molecular motion and are traditionally referred to as the four primordial elements of earth, water, air and fire.

4.3.9.4 *The Parts of the Body*

4.3.9.5 *The Cemetery Contemplations*

4.3.9.6 *Mindfulness of Breathing*

4.3.9.7 The first two of these different ways of contemplating the body (4.3.9.1 and 4.3.9.2) are especially suited to the practice of *vipassanā* and I shall reserve them for discussion in chapter 6. Of the other four, two are simply variants of two main meditation subjects that are considered under separate headings: the cemetery contemplations correspond to the ten kinds of body decay (section 4.2 above), and the contemplation of the elements to the analysis of the four elements (section 4.5 below). Mindfulness of breathing, because of its considerable importance as an insight exercise, is taken as a separate meditation subject with its own discipline and characteristics, as will be seen in section 4.3.10. This leaves for consideration now the exercise on the parts of the body.

In this exercise the meditator concentrates his attention successively (following a specific order) on thirty-two different parts of the body, defined for this purpose in the formula according to which he

reviews this body, up from the soles of the feet and down from the top of the hair, and contained in the skin, as full of many kinds of filth, and thinks: 'In this body there are head hairs, body hairs, nails, teeth, skin, flesh, sinews, bones, bonemarrow, brain, kidneys, heart, liver, pleura, spleen, lungs, bowels, mesentery, gorge, faeces, bile, phlegm, pus, blood, sweat, solid fat, tears, liquid fat, spittle, snot, synovial fluid, urine. . . .'[66]

There are detailed descriptions of the composition, location and appearance of each part.

The exercise begins with the list of the thirty-two parts being recited, first aloud and then mentally. Attention is then focused successively on each part, giving close consideration (following the corresponding standard description) to its colour, shape, position and relation to neighbouring organs. This is an exercise which combines visualizations with the direct perception of body sensations. Its purpose is to develop awareness of the compounded and impersonal nature of the organism, and of the perishable and often repulsive nature of the materials of which it is composed.

4.3.10 *Mindfulness of Breathing (ānāpānasati)*

Mindfulness applied to the body is, as has just been pointed out, one of the most fruitful areas of meditation practice. Mindfulness of breathing is generally considered as the most important of body mindfulness exercises, being particularly suitable as a subject of meditation both for the development of tranquillity (*samatha*) and of insight (*vipassanā*).

The reason for this lies in the fact that the process of breathing is simple, easily perceived and constantly available, which makes it an ideal meditation subject. Breathing, in addition to providing – like other bodily sensations – an immediately available sensory input, has the obvious advantages of being very easily perceived (the touch of air in the nostrils on breathing in and out) and of being available at all times and in any situation. Moreover, perception through the bodily sense of touch is more direct and immediate than that obtained through visual observation (as in the *kasiṇas* and the contemplations of body decay) and, of course, much more so than the purely mental perceptions of reflective exercises, which consist in observing mental constructs.

It is therefore no accident that this is precisely the exercise which the Buddha himself used to achieve concentration on the night which crowned his endeavours to obtain enlightenment, and explains why he repeatedly recommended it as being particularly suitable for all kinds of persons in all kinds of circumstances:

This concentration through mindfulness of breathing, assiduously developed and practised, is both peaceful and sublime, it is an unadulterated blissful abiding and it banishes at once, and stills, evil and unprofitable thoughts as soon as they arise.[67]

The exercise consists in focusing one's attention on the tip of the nose and the upper lip immediately underneath the nostrils, paying attention to the touch sensation of the air as one breathes in and out. *There must be no attempt at controlling breathing.* This is not a Yoga breathing exercise, but an exercise in focusing mindfulness. The breath must be allowed to come and go spontaneously. The only thing that has to be done is to observe with the closest possible attention the exact sensation produced by the air as it moves in and out through the nostrils, following with uninterrupted attention the full course of each in-breath and each out-breath. It is very important to ensure that one's attention remains focused on the nose only. There must be no attempt to follow the movement of the air inside the body (throat, lungs, etc.). The learning sign (see section 3 above) consists in the clear, steady awareness of the place where the air strikes:

These in-breaths and out-breaths occur striking the tip of the nose in a long-nosed man, and the upper lip in a short-nosed man. So he should fix the sign thus: 'This is the place where they strike.' [The counterpart sign, on the other hand,] is not the same for all; on the contrary, some say that when it appears it does so to certain people producing a light touch, like cotton or silk-cotton or a draught of air. But this is the exposition given in the commentaries: it appears to some like a star or a cluster of gems or a cluster of pearls, to others with a rough touch like that of silk-cotton seeds, or a peg made of heartwood, to others like a long braided string or a wreath of flowers or a puff of smoke, to others like a stretched-out cobweb or a film of cloud or a lotus flower or a chariot wheel or the moon's disc or the sun's disc.[68]

4.4 *Perception of Repulsiveness in Nutriment*

This can be regarded as complementary to the contemplations of the ten kinds of body decay and of the parts of the body. Like them, it aims at correcting blind complacency in relation to material things and attachment to the satisfaction of physical needs and desires.

When a monk devotes himself to this perception of repulsiveness in nutriment, his mind retreats, retracts and recoils from craving for flavours. He nourishes himself with nutriment without vanity.[69]

This exercise combines both the perceptual and reflective modes to focus attention on the disagreeable and repulsive aspects of food. It includes the clear perception, followed by appropriate reflection, of the trouble and effort involved in getting one's food, and sometimes even hardship and abuse (as in the case of a *bhikkhu*, or Buddhist monk, who on his almsround may be received 'with harsh words such as: "go away, you bald-head" '[70]), how easily food spoils and becomes off-putting; and how repulsive, as soon as we start thinking about them in detail, are to our minds the processes of chewing, swallowing, digesting, moving one's bowels, etc.

As he reviews repulsiveness in this way, physical nutriment becomes evident to him in its repulsive aspect. He cultivates that sign[71] again and again, develops and repeatedly practises it. As he does so, the hindrances[72] are suppressed and his mind is concentrated in access concentration.[73]

4.5 *Analysis of the Four Elements*

This, also known as the 'reflection on the material elements' or, as the *Visuddhi Magga* puts it, 'the definition of the four elements', is an exercise addressed to the consideration of the four primordial elements (already briefly referred to under 4.3.9.3 above as one of the variants of mindfulness of the body), earth, water, fire and air. Here the elements are not inspected individually in their own characteristic form (as is done in the corresponding *kasiṇas*), but rather by contemplating the various parts of the body and developing awareness of the fact that they are composed of the primordial elements in varying proportions. It should be recalled, of course, that in the philosophies of antiquity, both Western and Eastern, 'Earth', 'Water', 'Fire' and 'Air' did not merely denote earth, water, fire and air as perceived in everyday life, but that these terms stood for the basic modes in which matter is manifested, i.e. solidity, fluidity, radiation and vibration. According to molecular physics, these four states of matter are simply four points on a continuous scale which goes from the highest degree of molecular cohesion – the solid state ('Earth') – to the minimum degree – radiation ('Fire'). This is a reflective type of exercise, or recollection, which aims to achieve the mental experience of matter at the molecular level.

In passing it may be noted that some of the other exercises of body contemplation that have been mentioned, in particular the mindfulness of the body and mindfulness of breathing (which, it will be recalled, are of fundamental importance for the development of insight), go even further, in that their aim is to develop direct perception of material processes (and of accompanying mental processes) not only at the molecular level, but down to the play of fleeting, but highly energized atomic and even subatomic events. It is in this manner that there is a gradual revelation of *anicca*, i.e. of the impermanent, constantly changing nature of all that appears solid and lasting to the untrained mind.

But to return to the analysis of the four elements: the basic instructions are taken from the famous *Discourse on the Foundations of Mindfulness* (the basic text for the practice of *vipassanā*, which is considered in detail in chapter 6) and explain that the meditator

reflects upon this very body, however it be placed or disposed, with regard to its primary elements: 'there are in this body the earth element, the water element, the fire element, and the air element'. As if a skilful butcher or his apprentice, having slaughtered a cow and divided it into portions, were sitting at the junction of four high-roads, just so a monk reflects upon this very body, however it be placed or disposed, with regard to its primary elements.[74]

The *Visuddhi Magga* explains this comparison with a butcher thus:

Just as the butcher, while feeding the cow, bringing it to the slaughterhouse, keeping it tied up after bringing it there, slaughtering it, and seeing it slaughtered and dead, does not lose the perception 'cow', so long as he has not carved it up and divided it into parts; but when he has divided it up and is sitting there, he loses the perception 'cow' and the perception 'meat' occurs, he does not think 'I am selling cow' or 'they are carrying cow away', but rather, he thinks 'I am selling meat' or 'they are carrying meat away'; so too this monk, while still a foolish ordinary person . . . does not lose the perception 'living being' or 'man' or 'person' so long as he does not, by resolution of the compact into elements, review this body, however placed, however disposed, as consisting of elements. But when he does review it as consisting of elements, he loses the perception 'living being' and his mind establishes itself upon elements.[75]

The methodical approach to this exercise (especially recommended for, as the *Visuddhi Magga* puts it, 'one of not over-quick understanding') consists in considering the various parts and organic processes of one's body from the point of view of the element which is predominant in them; for instance, earth element (solidity) – nails, teeth, bones, sinews, etc.; water element (fluidity) – blood, bile, spittle, urine, etc.; fire element (radiation) – 'whatever there is internally in oneself that is fire, fiery, clung to, that is to say, that whereby one is warmed, ages, and burns up, and whereby what is eaten, drunk, chewed and tasted gets completely digested . . .';[76] air element (vibration) – the air in one's lungs, wind in the stomach and bowels, etc. In addition, there is a whole range of variants in which, while starting always from the concrete fact of the parts of the body and the processes which take place in it, reflective meditation is addressed more particularly to the conditions, characteristics, functions and manifestations of the elements, or states, as impersonal events. By practising this contemplation with careful discernment the meditator finds that 'the elements become evident to him under each [impersonal] heading. As he again and again adverts and gives attention to them, access concentration arises', and the meditator 'who is devoted to the defining of the four elements immerses himself in voidness and eliminates the perception of "living beings" '.[77]

4.6 *The Four Sublime States*

These four 'sublime states' of mind (literally, 'divine abidings' – *brahma vihāra*) are recollections which, like all the other exercises, can usefully be practised to achieve concentration. Their main significance, however, lies in the development of the meditator's moral and spiritual qualities, since they consist in the cultivation of what might be called the four cardinal virtues of Buddhism: loving kindness (or universal love), compassion, sympathetic joy and equanimity. Of course, the other meditative exercises correctly performed cannot but have positive effects on the mentality and character of the meditator and, to that extent, they can all be said to help in developing these virtues. The difference lies in the fact that in these particular exercises it is the specific virtues themselves which constitute the subjects for reflective contemplation. These recollections are therefore particularly useful in maintaining and perfecting the moral discipline (*sīla*) which, as has been repeatedly stressed, is indispensable for the practice of meditation. In addition, we shall see later (chapter 8) how these exercises fit in with the practice of both tranquillity and insight meditation for a better balance in the meditator

49

(both internally and in his interactions with others), and how they are thus a very important element of progress.

These are then essentially reflective exercises, based on the recollection of the positive qualities and advantages inherent in the virtues and of the dangers and harm to oneself and others resulting from their absence. It is characteristic of these exercises that the reflective realization of these points is accompanied by a positive volition, i.e. by a sustained effort of the will to develop attitudes and states of mind impregnated with the particular virtue which is the meditation subject.

The first three exercises are very similar. This is not surprising, bearing in mind that, in fact, they represent three aspects or modes of the same kind of mentality, whose essential characteristic is an outgoing, warm-hearted attitude towards others, without distinctions between 'yours' and 'mine'. *Mettā* (central to Buddhism both as concept and experience), which is usually translated as 'loving kindness', is 'charity' in the original sense of the word, that is to say, the disinterested love of one's fellows which moves one to seek their good and happiness without desiring anything for oneself; compassion (*karuṇā*) and sympathetic joy (*muditā*) are the evident and mutually complementary manifestations of loving kindness: the ever present readiness to share the sufferings and the joys of others.

4.6.1 *Loving Kindness (*mettā*)*

This meditation begins with a consideration intended to strengthen one's motivation. One starts by considering the harmfulness of hate and the benefits of tolerance and understanding. After this preliminary consideration, the exercise proper consists in cultivating loving kindness towards all beings, following a specific order which is based on sound psychological considerations.

First of all there are four categories of persons which, to begin with, should not be taken as subjects for the exercise of loving kindness, and this for obvious psychological reasons. The categories to be avoided are an antipathetic person (because of the difficulty, for a beginner, in overcoming one's instinctive dislike), a dearly loved friend (because of the excessive emotional involvement that the relationship implies), someone to whom we are entirely indifferent (because of the difficulty in developing sufficient interest), and someone with whom we are on actively hostile terms (because of the excessive negative emotional involvement). One should also refrain from developing loving kindness specifically towards the opposite sex (to avoid the craving and clinging inherent in sexual involvement) and towards a dead person (as no truly valid relationship can be developed with someone who is no longer there).

But, one may well ask at this point, what is left once you have excluded all those you like, all those you dislike, and all those you do not care about either way? The answer, of course, is oneself. And this is, in fact, precisely where one begins.

> First of all, loving kindness should be developed only towards oneself, doing it repeatedly thus: 'May I be happy and free from suffering', or 'May I keep myself free from enmity, affliction and anxiety, and live happily'[78]

or by means of similar formulations. At first sight, this business of starting with oneself may seem a very strange way of going about developing love for others. However, it must be noted that the *Visuddhi Magga* takes good care to specify that in this initial exercise the meditator must be clear that he is taking himself as an example of a sentient being. He represents *any* being, and *all* beings:

> If he develops it in this way: 'I am happy. Just as I want to be happy and dread pain, as I want to live and not to die, so do other beings, too', making himself the example, then desire for other beings' welfare and happiness arises in him. And this method is indicated by the Blessed One's saying:

> > I visited all quarters with my mind
> > nor found I any dearer than myself;
> > self is likewise to every other dear;
> > who loves himself will never harm another.[79]

A moment's reflection will show that this way of beginning the exercise is based on two excellent psychological principles. First, that happiness or unhappiness is a state of mind, that is to say, it is something which depends essentially on oneself. It should be carefully noted that the formula used for the exercise does not speak in terms of getting something or getting rid of something in order to be happy, but in terms of keeping oneself free, internally, from enmity, affliction and anxiety (which, it must be well noted, are *not* things outside ourselves as part of the environment, but simply our own reactions to the environment), and thus to be happy because one is at peace with oneself, whatever the circumstances. Secondly, and equally self-evident, to be at peace with others one has to begin by being at peace with, and in, oneself. This is a principle well recognized and much used in modern psychotherapy: 'Make friends with yourself.' Indeed, if one is upset by feelings of anger, hate or anxiety, one is simply not in a position to show genuine benevolence towards others. True loving kindness is not a matter of benevolent outward behaviour (while keeping internal negativities more or less successfully under control), but of the spontaneous caring outflow of a tranquil mind. It is therefore obvious that you must begin by being loving to yourself before you can be loving to others.

'Who loves himself, will never harm another' – that is the crucial point. A Western reader is immediately reminded of the famous injunction by that other great teacher, Jesus Christ: 'Thou shalt love thy neighbour as thyself.' The difference in formulation, however, is significant. In the Western tradition an *obligation* is placed upon us from the outside: 'Thou *shalt*'. In the Buddha's teaching we are advised that a given course of action will produce a given state of affairs. There is no question of obligation.

It must be quite clearly understood that loving kindness has nothing to do with facile indulgence or emotional wallowing. Genuine loving kindness is perfectly clearsighted and does not ignore or overlook the faults and defects in its objects. It is fully conscious acceptance, not ignorance, an acceptance which is the outward manifestation of an internal state of peace and balance, and which is thus not motivated by desire, selfishness, clinging or delusion.

Once mental concentration has been achieved with loving kindness directed at the meditator himself, the loving kindness thus developed should be directed to pervade other subjects. The next step, 'in order to proceed easily' says the *Visuddhi Magga*, should be

such gifts, kind words, etc., as inspire love and endearment, such virtue, learning, etc., as inspire respect and reverence, met with in a teacher or his equivalent, or a preceptor or his equivalent, developing loving kindness towards him in the way beginning: 'May this good man be happy and free from suffering.'[80]

Thereafter one may proceed to the more difficult subjects (those which had to be avoided to begin with) in this order: a very dear friend, a neutral person, an antipathetic or hostile person (these need not be the same each time; on different occasions, different individuals may be selected within each category).[81]

Practising assiduously in this manner, going regularly through the sequence as indicated, sooner or later the mental state may be attained which is known as 'the breaking down of the barriers'. This is a state of total, balanced openness, in which the meditator accomplishes 'mental impartiality towards the four persons, that is to say himself, the dear person, the neutral person and the hostile person'. The breaking down of the barriers is the equivalent of the counterpart sign in perceptual exercises and denotes the achievement of access concentration. In chapter 8 we see how loving kindness, developed on the basis of specific individuals, may be expanded until it becomes a universal pervasion of all beings.

4.6.2 *Compassion (* karuṇā) *and Sympathetic Joy (*muditā)

Since these two virtues are, in effect, special aspects of loving kindness, the relative exercises are similar in nature, the only differences springing from the specific character of the virtue. One important difference is that one starts at once with someone else, not with oneself – naturally enough, since compassion and sympathy, being partial aspects of loving kindness, might easily become self-pity and self-congratulation.

In the exercise of compassion one should begin with some obvious case of suffering and misfortune (provided that it does not concern a close friend – which might upset us too much – or someone whom we definitely dislike – in which case it might be difficult to generate genuine compassion). The attitude to be developed is: 'This being has indeed been reduced to misery; if only he could be freed from this suffering.' If one does not encounter such a person, one may also take the case of someone who appears to be happy and well off but whose character and behaviour are manifestly undesirable, and compassion should then be aroused by thinking that, although apparently happy and successful, that person is really a poor wretch because, by his failure to perform any good deeds in body, speech or mind, he is preparing for himself untold misery at a later stage. Having thus aroused compassion for the first subject, one should then proceed – as in the loving-kindness exercise – by turning successively to a dear person, a neutral person and a hostile one.

The sympathetic-joy exercise should begin with someone one knows and likes well but with whom one is not too closely involved. The important thing is that the person should be of a happy and cheerful disposition, whose demonstrative gladness and good humour can easily be shared. Then, as in the other cases, the exercise continues with dear, neutral and hostile persons.

In these two exercises of compassion and sympathetic joy one should also persevere until access concentration by 'breaking down the barriers' is achieved; their pervasion can then also be extended to all beings.

4.6.3 *Equanimity (*upekkhā)

The procedure is similar to the previous ones, but beginning with a neutral person and then moving successively to a dear person and to a hostile one. There is, however, an important difference which sets this exercise apart not only from the three previous sublime states but also from all those we have so far seen in this chapter. The difference lies in the fact that this is a very advanced concentration exercise which presupposes the prior achievement – by means of one of the other three sublime states as meditation subjects – of the level of concentration and tranquillity known as the third absorption (or third *jhāna*), but which cannot itself be used to attain any of the first three absorptions. In other words, it can only be used to achieve the fourth absorption, as is shown in chapter 5. Both equanimity and loving kindness, however, are of particular relevance to the progress of insight, being part both of the means to liberation and of its end manifestations. They will accordingly be considered at greater length in this connection in chapter 8.

4.7 *The Four Immaterial States*

These are the experiential states of *boundless space*, *boundless consciousness*, *nothingness* and *neither-perception-nor-non-perception*. They require the most advanced levels of concentration and belong exclusively to the practice of tranquillity meditation, representing the achievement of the highest possible degrees of mental absorption, or what is known as 'the absorptions at the formless levels' (*arūpa jhāna*), sometimes also called 'immaterial absorptions'. They will therefore be considered in the chapter on *samatha*, being mentioned at this point only for the sake of completing the overview of traditional meditation subjects in this chapter.

Before attempting these exercises it is necessary to have attained the four basic degrees of mental absorption in *samatha*, i.e. 'the absorptions at the formal levels' (*rūpa jhāna*, also known as 'fine-material absorptions'), using for this purpose any one of the *kasiṇas* with the exception of 'limited space'. After the fourth basic absorption has been achieved with a *kasiṇa*, the meditator goes on refining and intensifying concentration even further by discarding the *kasiṇa* and its sign and focusing only on the space which was occupied by the *kasiṇa*. In this manner access concentration is established with space (which is, in itself, unbounded) as the *counterpart sign*, which represents a higher degree of abstraction than that of the fourth absorption.

The procedure is similar for each of the other three 'formless' or 'immaterial' absorptions, each one of them starting with the previous one as its basis. Thus, after achieving the contemplation of *boundless space*, one proceeds by discarding it and concentrating attention on the existing awareness of that space, developing in this manner the contemplation of *boundless consciousness*. Proceeding to an even more rare-fied stage, the awareness itself can be discarded, and the basis for contemplation is then the nonexistence of the previous consciousness. This is the contemplation of *nothingness*. As the awareness of *nothingness* (which sounds paradoxical, but is an experiential fact) is established, the degree of withdrawal from perception and of mental abstraction becomes such that the resulting state can no longer be said to involve any perception or awareness in the ordinary sense of the terms. At the same time, however, the mental condition is *not* one of simple unconsciousness. This is what is described as the state of *neither-perception-nor-non-perception*, which is the fourth immaterial state (corresponding to the fourth of the formless absorptions).

4.8 This concludes the brief survey of the forty meditation subjects used to develop mental concentration in the Buddhist tradition. From among these an experienced teacher will select in each case the subject best suited to the character, abilities and circumstances of a given student, as well as to the intended course of training, i.e. whether the aim is to develop tranquillity (*samatha*) or insight (*vipassanā*), or a combination of both.

5
Samatha – *Development of Tranquillity*

1 As explained in chapter 3, the purpose of *samatha* meditation is the achievement of altered states of consciousness characterized by a high degree of tranquillity and mental peace. In that same chapter it is also explained that this purpose can be achieved by developing progressively higher levels of mental concentration, gradually discarding all sensory and raciocinative inputs. This is why it was said that this is an *abstractive* kind of meditation which goes systematically through successive stages of mental absorption which are increasingly devoid of sense percepts and mental discourse.

The successive practice of *samatha* exercises requires (even more than that of *vipassanā*, which will be considered in the next chapter) the regular personal supervision of a qualified master, if frustrations, errors and confusion are to be avoided. There is, therefore, not much that can be said about *samatha* practice in a written introduction such as this, except to give a general, and purely theoretical, idea of what it is about and of how the various stages fit in with one another. This is all that the following pages attempt to do: to draw a sketchy map of a complex terrain.

2 *The Absorptions (*jhāna)

2.1 *Samatha* meditation, the Buddhist meditation of tranquillity, is traditionally regarded as comprising eight progressive stages of mental abstraction or absorption, known as *jhānas* (*jhāna*, in Pali, means literally 'meditation' or 'contemplation').[82]

As already outlined when referring to the immaterial states at the end

56

of the previous chapter, these eight absorptions are divided into two main groups: the four basic degrees of mental absorption, often referred to in English as 'fine-material' absorptions, but which are better described as *formal absorptions (rūpa jhāna)*; and the four additional degrees, known as 'immaterial' or *formless absorptions (arūpa jhāna)*.

The starting point for the formal absorptions is the achievement of *access concentration*,[83] established on the basis of a given meditation subject and developed subsequently until the *concentration of attainment* (or *fixed concentration*)[84] is reached. In the latter, it will be remembered, attention becomes fully absorbed in the counterpart sign[85] developed on the basis of the initial subject, and it is at this point that the attainment of the basic absorptions begins. The additional degrees are developed in a similar manner, also going through the stages of access and fixed concentration, but their starting point (as already mentioned in chapter 4, section 4.7 above) is the fourth basic absorption, attained by means of a *kasiṇa* as the meditation subject. In this connection it should be remembered that not all of the forty meditation subjects are suitable for all purposes; some of them may be used to develop both access and attainment concentration, while others can only go as far as the access level.

Those that lead only to access are ten – the eight reflective recollection exercises, plus the perception of repulsiveness in nutriment and the analysis of the four elements (see chapter 4, sections 4.3–4.5). These can be used simply as beneficial mental exercises (since access concentration is already, in itself, a very positive experience of heightened consciousness) or, of course, for the practice of insight meditation.

The other thirty meditation subjects are all suitable for the establishment of fixed, or attainment, concentration and may therefore be used for the practice of both insight (*vipassanā*) and tranquillity (*samatha*). Let us note in passing that two of them, mindfulness of breathing and mindfulness of the body, are particularly useful at the access level for the practice of insight (see chapter 6). At this point, however, we are concerned with the development of tranquillity, and here it should be noted that not all of these can lead to the attainment of all the levels of absorption just mentioned. The ten kinds of body decay, as well as the mindfulness of the body, lead only to the first absorption. The first three of the four sublime states (loving kindness, compassion and sympathetic joy) can be used to attain levels up to the third absorption. The ten *kasiṇas* and mindfulness of breathing produce all four basic absorptions. The fourth sublime state (equanimity) is suitable only for the fourth absorption and, as will be recalled (chapter 4, section 4.6.3), cannot be used to establish access concentration, which must be previously obtained by means of one of the other sublime states. The four immaterial states, finally, starting from the fourth basic absorption (achieved by means of any one of the ten *kasiṇas*, with the exception of 'limited space'), lead to the successive attainment of the fifth, sixth, seventh and eighth absorptions (that is to say, the four formless bases).

I shall now briefly outline each of the eight absorptions to give a summary idea of the kinds of states they involve and of how one works towards their attainment. For this purpose I shall take the standard definitions of the absorptions as found in many passages of the Buddha's *Discourses* and comment upon them with the help of references and elucidations from the *Visuddhi Magga*.

2.2 Formal or 'Fine-Material' Absorptions (rūpa jhāna)

The initial meditative procedure is always the same: attention must first be focused on the meditation subject (*preparatory concentration*), then steadied and intensified (going through the successive stages of (a) conscious and exclusive attention to the subject, which is the 'preliminary sign', (b) the 'learning sign' and (c) the 'counterpart sign' – see chapter 4, sections 3.1–3.3) until *access concentration* is achieved. Then, for the development of *samatha*, the meditator goes on strengthening and refining mental concentration on the basis of the counterpart sign that has been established, until *fixed* or *attainment concentration* is achieved.

2.2.1 First Absorption

Working in this manner, the meditator 'quite secluded from sense desires, secluded from unprofitable things, enters upon and dwells in the first absorption, which is accompanied by applied and sustained thought, with happiness and bliss born of seclusion.[86]

The definition specifies that the meditator is 'quite secluded from sense desires' because the mind is concentrating exclusively on the counterpart sign established on the basis of the initial meditation subject. 'Secluded from unprofitable things' means that the meditator at that time is free from what are known in the Buddhist tradition as the 'five hindrances' which, when present, confuse the mind and hinder progress. They are sense desires, ill will, sloth and torpor, agitation and worry, and sceptical doubt. There can be no progress as long as the meditator is not free from these hindrances. This is why it is stated that the first absorption is 'born of seclusion'. To the extent that there is successful progress in concentration, from the preliminary focusing of the mind to the level of access, the mind is, quite naturally, freed from these hindrances (if one is *really* concentrating on the meditation subject, there is no room at the same time for feelings of desire, ill will, sloth, and so on).[87] Conversely, the more often and more completely the mind is cleared from hindrances, the better and more effectively it concentrates. It is a process of continuous positive feedback.

The distinctive characteristics of the first absorption (which are the same both in a beginner's first momentary attainment and in the more lasting states achieved by experienced meditators) are 'happiness and bliss' and the fact that the condition 'is accompanied by applied and sustained thought'. The latter qualification makes it clear that the first level of absorption still comprises elements of reflection and mental discourse: thoughts arise (applied thought) and are pursued (sustained thought). However, these reflective activities are strictly integrated in the meditative process and serve to strengthen it. *Applied thought* consists of applying or focusing the thinking capacity of the mind exclusively on the meditation subject (and on the counterpart sign once this has arisen), while *sustained thought* means maintaining the reflective activity steady on the subject, without distractions. The *Visuddhi Magga* illustrates this operation with the similes of a bell, a bird and a bee. *Applied thought* is like the first striking of a bell; *sustained thought* is like the continued ringing of the bell; *applied thought* is 'like a bird's spreading out its wings when about to soar into the air, and like a bee's diving towards a lotus flower when it is minded to follow up the scent of it'; while *sustained thought* is 'like the bird's planing with outspread wings after soaring into the air, and like the bee's buzzing above the lotus after it has dived towards it.'[88]

The reference to 'happiness and bliss' is of particular importance as characterizing the positive nature of the state of consciousness attained in this first absorption (as well as in the next one, as we shall see shortly). These terms, too, are used in highly specific, technical senses in Buddhist meditation: *happiness*[89] is 'the contentedness at getting a desirable object', and *bliss*[90] is 'the actual experiencing of it when got'. To clarify this the *Visuddhi Magga* explains that 'if a man exhausted in a desert saw or learnt about a pond on the edge of a wood, he would have happiness; but if he went into the wood's shade and used the water, he would have bliss.'[91]

Happiness plays a very important part already in the preliminary stages, while approaching and attaining the level of access to the absorption. In fact, when the meditator is endeavouring to develop concentration, happiness is both the positive fruit of his first deliberate, well-disciplined efforts and a motivation to further effort and progress. The manifestations of happiness vary in kind, degree and duration. Traditional terminology[92] distinguishes the following: *minor happiness*, which is like a shiver 'raising the hairs on the body'; *momentary happiness* is 'like flashes of lightning at different moments'; *showering happiness* 'breaks over the body again and again, like waves on the seashore'; *uplifting happiness* is manifested not only as mental uplift, but also as producing a physical sensation of extreme lightness, as if one were floating on air; finally, the *pervading* (or *rapturous*) *happiness* is when 'the whole body is completely pervaded, like a filled bladder, or like a rock cavern invaded by a huge inundation.'

At this point, it is worth quoting a whole passage from the *Visuddhi Magga* which briefly describes the sequence of psychosomatic conditions which characterize progress from the initial focusing on the meditation subject to the attainment of absorption:

Now this fivefold happiness,[93] when conceived and matured, perfects the twofold tranquillity, that is, bodily and mental tranquillity. When tranquillity is conceived and matured, it perfects the twofold bliss, that is, bodily and mental bliss. When bliss is conceived and matured, it perfects the threefold concentration, that is, momentary concentration,[94] access concentration and attainment concentration. Of these, the root of attainment concentration is pervading happiness which, as it grows, is associated with concentration.[95]

The characteristics of the first absorption can best be summed up in the Buddha's own words:

The first absorption is free from five things, and possesses five things. Indeed, monks, in him who has attained the first absorption there is no sense desire, no ill-will, no sloth and torpor, no agitation and worry, and no doubt.[96] He dwells concentrated, happy and blissful, exercising applied and sustained thought.[97]

Let us now turn to the phrase in the formula which specifies that the meditator 'enters upon and dwells in the first absorption'. Here it should be noted that, when attaining this state for the first time, a meditator usually does not manage to remain in it for more than a few moments (this is the momentary attainment) and returns almost at once to the level of access. With practice, however, one develops an increasing facility for entering into full absorption and for remaining, or dwelling, in it for longer and longer periods. In this manner full control is eventually achieved, which consists in the ability to enter upon the first absorption at any time and to remain in it for as long as one wishes (this is the stable attainment). It is rather like learning to ride a bicycle. At the beginning one keeps on falling off but, with practice, keeping one's balance on two wheels becomes second nature. This learning process is the same for all the absorptions, that is to say, normally attainment is momentary in the beginning and is gradually perfected until full mastery is achieved.[98]

2.2.2 Extending the Sign

The process of stabilizing and intensifying abstractive concentration can be greatly aided by an exercise known as 'extending the sign'. This is useful both for this first level of absorption that we are now considering, as well as for the other three basic absorptions, and a variant thereof is – as will be seen later – essential for the attainment of the fifth absorption (i.e. the absorption of the first formless base).

This exercise is practised on the basis of any one of the *kasiṇas* (with the exception of 'limited space') and consists in mentally extending, by successive stages, the counterpart sign that has been originally developed, so that it is mentally expanded to comprise larger and larger areas. This is how the *Visuddhi Magga* illustrates the extension exercise on the basis of the earth *kasiṇa* (whose counterpart sign, it will be recalled, is characterized by images of brightness and purity: 'like a looking-glass disc . . . , like a mother-of-pearl disc . . . , like the moon's disc'). According to the manual, the meditator should proceed as follows:

> He should first delimit with his mind successive sizes for the sign, as acquired, that is to say, one finger, two fingers, three fingers, four fingers, and then extend it by the amount delimited, just as a ploughman delimits with the plough the area to be ploughed and then ploughs within the area delimited . . . . He should not extend it without having delimited [the area to be covered]. After that has been done, he can further extend it, doing so by delimiting successive boundaries of say one span, two spans, the verandah, the surrounding space, the monastery, and the boundaries of the village, the town, the district, the kingdom, and the ocean, or making even the extreme limit the world sphere or even beyond.[99]

2.2.3 Reviewing

In the practice of *samatha* the passage from one absorption to the next is not a continuous process. There are breaks between each absorption. When a meditator has entered upon the first absorption,[100] before proceeding to the second one he needs to emerge from the first and mentally review and assess the experience he has just lived. The same applies to the transition from the second to the third absorptions, from the third to the fourth, and so on. This is called 'reviewing' in traditional terminology, since what the meditator has to do is to review with scrupulous care and deliberation the distinguishing characteristics of the level of absorption he has just experienced so as to establish its precise quality. This review reveals what is still susceptible of improvement at each level and strengthens the motivation to work towards the next.

In the case of the first absorption, the *Visuddhi Magga* says that, once the meditator has mastered it,

on emerging from the now familiar first absorption, he can regard the flaws in it in this way: 'This attainment is threatened by the nearness of the hindrances,[101] and its factors are weakened by the grossness of the applied and sustained thought.'[102] He can bring the second absorption to mind, as quieter, and so end his attachment to the first absorption and set about doing what is needed for attaining the second. When he has emerged from the first, applied and sustained thought appear gross to him as he reviews the absorption factors with mindfulness and full awareness, while happiness and bliss and unification of mind [i.e. concentration] appear peaceful.

Then the meditator concentrates the mind once again, using either the same meditation subject as for the first absorption or another suitable one, goes through the usual stages of learning sign–counterpart sign–access concentration–attainment concentration (a process which can take place very quickly as one's skill develops), and enters upon the second absorption. The technique for achieving concentration is, of course, the same as before, but the difference lies in the meditator's motivation, which is now different from the previous one because it is based on the actual experience of the first absorption, the possibilities which it has revealed, the analysis of the experience carried out in the subsequent review, and the resulting motivation to advance to the second absorption. As the *Visuddhi Magga* goes on to explain:

Then, as he brings that same sign to mind . . . again and again, *with the purpose of abandoning the gross factors* [i.e. applied and sustained thought] *and obtaining the peaceful factors* [which are happiness, bliss and unification of mind] he knows: 'Now the second absorption will arise' [my *underlining*].[103]

2.2.4 *Second Absorption*

With the stilling of applied and sustained thought, he enters upon and dwells in the second absorption, which has internal confidence and singleness of mind, without applied thought, without sustained thought, with happiness and bliss born of concentration.[104]

Of this absorption it is said that 'it abandons two factors and possesses three factors'.[105] The two factors abandoned are, of course, the reflective functions of applied and sustained thought. The three factors which are present are happiness, bliss and singleness or unification of mind, i.e. concentration. Internal confidence is not considered as an additional factor since it is simply the consequence of the other three.

One difference to be noted between the first and the second absorptions is that the latter is said to be 'born of concentration', while the former was 'born of seclusion'. What this means is that, as already mentioned in connection with the first absorption, the process of concentrating the mind has to begin by removing the negative states of mind known as hindrances; this is the meaning of 'seclusion', i.e. the mind is isolated from the hindrances. When working towards the second absorption, on the other hand, the meditator already enjoys the advantages resulting from the degree of concentration attained in the first. This is why it is said that the second absorption is 'born of concentration'.

Once the second absorption has been mastered, the procedure for emerging from it and entering upon the third is – as already indicated – similar to that which was described for the transition from the first to the second. The next factor to be shed at this point is that of 'happiness'.

On emerging from the now familiar second absorption, he can regard the flaws in it in this way: 'This attainment is threatened by the nearness of applied and sustained thought, whatever there is in it of happiness, of mental excitement, proclaims its grossness, and its factors are weakened by the grossness of the happiness so expressed.'[106] He can bring the third absorption to mind, as quieter, and so end his attachment to the second absorption and set about doing what is needed for attaining the third. When he has emerged from the second absorption, happiness appears gross to him, as he reviews the absorption factors with mindfulness and full awareness, while bliss and unification of mind appear peaceful.[107]

The meditator then proceeds to concentrate the mind once again, 'with the purpose of abandoning the gross factor [happiness] and obtaining the peaceful factors [bliss and unification of mind]' and perseveres thus until the third absorption is attained.

2.2.5 *Third Absorption*

With the fading away of happiness as well, he dwells equanimous, mindful and fully aware, experiencing bodily bliss, and enters upon and dwells in the third absorption, on account of which the Noble Ones declare: 'He dwells in bliss, who has equanimity and is mindful.'[108]

This absorption 'abandons one factor and possesses two factors'.[109] The factor abandoned is, as has just been seen, that of happiness, because it is something which, though pleasant, causes mental excitement and has thus an unsettling effect. The two remaining factors which characterize this level of absorption are bliss and unification of mind. At first sight the wording of the traditional formula may seem to include other elements as well, but closer inspection reveals that this is not the case. In fact, in the formula there is reference not only to bliss but also to equanimity, mindfulness and full awareness. As regards the last two, however, it can readily be appreciated that the terms 'mindful' and 'fully aware' (as well as the phrase 'is mindful' later on) are simply ways of describing concentration. Concentration, or unification of mind, is precisely this: to be entirely mindful (successively, of the meditation subject, the learning sign and the counterpart sign) with full awareness and comprehension of what is being done. The *Visuddhi Magga*, in order to stress this, says that

the subtlety of this absorption, which is due to the abandoning of the gross factors,[110] requires that the mind's going should always include the functions of mindfulness and full-awareness, like that of a man on a razor's edge.[111]

As for equanimity, what emerges at this level of absorption is a beginning of equanimity, which is considered as an integral part of the experience of bliss. It is obvious, of course, that equanimity, as a state of emotional and mental balance, is a blissful kind of experience. In fact, well-developed equanimity, characterized by an even, serene cast of mind, is a higher form of bliss. As will be seen in a moment, when a highly developed level of equanimity is attained in the fourth absorption, the experience is then no longer describable in terms of bliss or pleasure,[112] and this is therefore said to be the factor that is abandoned there.

In this third absorption, however, bliss, together with concentration, is still of fundamental importance, and its presence at the mental level is accompanied by an extremely pleasant feeling of wellbeing and ease at the physical level. This is why it is said that in the third absorption the meditator 'experiences bodily bliss'.

But in the dialectics of existence every coin has two sides: bliss and suffering, pleasure and pain, are inevitable counterparts. Hence a state of bliss, no matter how intensely pleasant and how prolonged, does not transcend the duality and is still very far from a state of perfection. In the traditional terminology, it is still 'gross'.[113] Thus, the meditator,

on emerging from the now familiar third absorption, can regard the flaws in it in this way: 'This attainment is threatened by the nearness of happiness, whatever there is in it of mental concern about bliss proclaims its grossness, and its factors are weakened by the grossness of the bliss so expressed.' He can bring the fourth absorption to mind, as quieter, and so end his attachment to the third absorption and set about doing what is needed for attaining the fourth. When he has emerged from the third absorption, the bliss, in other words, the mental joy, appears gross to him as he reviews the absorption factors with mindfulness and full awareness, while the equanimity as feeling and the unification of mind appear peaceful.

On this basis, the meditator starts working towards the fourth absorption,

with the purpose of abandoning the gross factor [specifically, bliss as mental joy, and also all pleasant bodily sensations associated with it] and obtaining the peaceful factors [equanimity and unification of mind].[114]

2.2.6 *Suitability of the Fourth Sublime State (Equanimity) for the Attainment of the Fourth Absorption*

As in the previous transitions (from the first to the second, and from the second to the third absorptions), concentration can again be developed either with the same meditation subject that was used previously or with any other suitable one, always taking into account the fact that not all subjects are suitable for the attainment of all levels of absorption (see section 2.1 of this chapter).

In the particular case of working towards the fourth absorption, however, there is one meditation subject which, by its very nature, is particularly suitable, in view of the fact that equanimity is one of the two essential factors in this absorption. The subject is, of course, the fourth sublime state which is, precisely, equanimity. It will also be recalled that (as indicated in chapter 4, section 4.6.3 and in section 2.1 of this chapter) this meditation subject can be used only for the attainment of the fourth absorption and not for the previous ones. The advantages of using as meditation subject one of the two factors which distinguish the state one wishes to attain are obvious. It must be remembered, however, that the use of equanimity as a meditation subject to attain the fourth absorption must be led up to by the use of one of the other three sublime states (rather than, for instance, a *kasiṇa*) for the attainment of the three preceding levels.

In fact, to be able to enter upon the fourth absorption using equanimity itself as the meditation subject, it is necessary that the third absorption should have been attained on the basis of loving kindness, compassion or sympathetic joy as meditation subjects. In this case the consideration of the flaws in the third absorption is done by seeing 'danger in the former three sublime states, because they are linked with attention given to beings' enjoyment in the way beginning "May they be happy", because resentment and approval are near, and because their association with joy is gross.'[115] (Equanimity as a meditation subject for the purpose of the fourth absorption is developed as explained in chapter 4, section 4.6.3.)

2.2.7 *Fourth Absorption*

With the abandoning of pleasure and pain and with the previous disappearance of joy and grief, he enters upon and dwells in the fourth absorption, which has neither pain nor pleasure and has purity of mindfulness due to equanimity.[116]

The last factor which had to be left behind for the purpose of this absorption was, as we just saw, bliss. It should not be surprising, however, that its 'abandoning' should now be expressed in terms of pleasure and pain, joy and grief. The point is that the state now being entered upon is one of well-established equanimity and, as such, is free from *all* valuation, either positive or negative, of *both* physical and mental data. As the *Visuddhi Magga* explains, 'pleasure and pain' mean 'bodily pleasure and bodily pain', and 'joy and grief' mean 'mental pleasure and mental pain'.[117] Thus the whole gamut is covered. As regards the last two, the manual further explains that they are referred to as having 'previously' disappeared because, in fact, they vanish already before the fourth absorption is actually entered upon. The disappearance of these mental factors precedes the establishment of the concentration of attainment of the fourth absorption. The physical factors, on the other hand, are relinquished as the absorption is entered upon, which is then said to have 'neither pain nor pleasure' (either mental or physical) and comprises only pure mindfulness due to equanimity. The *Visuddhi Magga* specifies that this important quality, though emerging fully only now, in the fourth absorption, is an essential part of the whole process of tranquillity development. 'This equanimity exists in the three lower absorptions too,' it says.

But, just as the moon is hardly visible during the day, even when riding high in the sky, because it is outshone by the sun's greater radiance, so too the equanimity which exists in the three lower absorptions is 'outshone by the glare' of the gross factors: it is present to some extent but not powerful enough not to be obscured by them.

It will be recalled that the gross factors are applied and sustained thought in the first absorption, happiness in the second, and bliss in the third. At each higher level the 'gross' factor is correspondingly less so (happiness tends to occupy the mind less than the exercise of applied and sustained thought, and bliss tends to involve less excitement than happiness). Pursuing the *Visuddhi Magga* image, one can say that the third absorption is like the moment of sundown, when the soft radiance of the moon begins to be discernible. This is why equanimity is, in fact, mentioned there for the first time ('he dwells in bliss, who has equanimity and is mindful'), even though it is not yet a main factor. With the fourth absorption, night has fallen; as the obscuring factors have disappeared, the moon of equanimity shines in its full purity, which is the purity of mindfulness. 'This is why,' concludes the *Visuddhi Magga*, 'only this absorption is said to have purity of mindfulness due to equanimity.'[118]

This fourth absorption, the last of the formal, or 'fine-material', ones, is distinguished, as can be seen, by a high degree of concentration and tranquillity. It constitutes the starting point for the four formless absorptions, which represent highly rarefied states of consciousness very far removed from those we are familiar with in any kind of everyday experience.

2.3 The Formless Absorptions (arūpa jhāna)

The practice of the four basic absorptions, even though it goes quite far in discarding sense percepts and mental stimuli, still involves a certain extent of material and formal elements – partly on account of the material nature of the subjects used for perceptual exercises (such as the *kasinas*, the body, its organs and component elements, breathing, etc.), partly because of the essentially concrete nature of reflective exercises (such as the contemplation of the qualities of the Buddha, the *Dhamma* and the *Sangha*, or the nature and effects of certain virtues, or the mental generation of sublime states – compassion, loving kindness, etc. – with specific individuals as objects) and, in any case, because of the mental activities and the states of mind and body which occur at those levels (applied and sustained thought, the various kinds of happiness, physical and mental bliss, etc.). This is why they are called *formal* or 'fine-material' absorptions.

The four additional levels of absorption, on the other hand, move forward to extremely subtle states of consciousness, leaving behind all the component elements, mental and physical, internal and external, of our accustomed human environment. This is why they are referred to as *formless* or 'immaterial' absorptions.

The necessary precondition for their development is, as already pointed out, the prior attainment of the basic, or formal absorptions up to the fourth, using as a meditation subject any one of the nine possible *kasiṇas*. Neither the tenth *kasiṇa* (limited space) nor any of the other thirty meditation subjects is suitable as a basis for proceeding towards the formless absorptions. The reason for this is that, since the aim here is to transcend even the subtlest aspects of the material world, it is necessary to begin precisely with a material subject, which is suitable for perceptual meditation, and then progressively discard all elements of materiality, as was shown in discussing the four immaterial states (chapter 4, section 4.7), each one of which, in fact, correlates with one of the formless absorptions and is the only suitable base for entering upon it.

Put more simply, only the nine *kasiṇas* (excluding 'limited space') can be used to develop the immaterial states, and only these states provide access to the formless absorptions. Let us once again turn to the *Visuddhi Magga* for an explanation.

2.3.1 *Fifth Absorption: First Formless Base (Boundless Space)*

The meditator who wants to develop this absorption considers the precarious and unsatisfactory nature of physical matter in all its forms, and of the perceptions relating thereto and, in order to transcend this situation,

he enters upon the fourth absorption in any one of the nine *kasiṇas* . . . omitting the limited-space *kasiṇa*. Now, although he has already surmounted gross physical matter by means of the fourth absorption of the formal sphere, nevertheless he still wants to surmount the material aspect of the *kasiṇa*, which is the counterpart [of the material sphere]. How does he do this? . . . On emerging from the now familiar fourth absorption . . . he sees the danger in it in this way: 'This makes its object the materiality with which I have become dissatisfied' and 'It has joy as its near enemy', and 'It is grosser than the peaceful liberations' [which is another name for the immaterial states]. . . . When he has seen the danger in that fourth absorption in this way and has ended his attachment to it, he gives his attention to the base consisting of boundless space, as peaceful.[119]

At this point the meditator starts working on whatever *kasiṇa* he has selected and proceeds to 'extend the *kasiṇa*' in the same manner as described above for extending the counterpart sign in connection with the formal absorptions (section 2.2.2 of this chapter), except that in this case the extension exercise is applied directly to the initial *kasiṇa*, i.e. to the actual object itself. The extension of the *kasiṇa* is followed by its elimination:

When he has spread out the *kasiṇa* to the limit of the world-sphere, or as far as he likes, he removes the *kasiṇa* [materiality] by giving his attention to the space touched by it, as "space" or "boundless space".'

The explanation adds that

removing the *kasiṇa* . . . is simply that the meditator does not advert to it, or give attention to it, or review it; it is when he neither adverts to it, nor gives attention to it, nor reviews it, but gives his attention exclusively to the space touched by it, as 'space, space' that he is said to 'remove the *kasiṇa*'.[120]

The meditator then proceeds to develop concentration, using as a sign the space left by the removal of the *kasiṇa*, until he attains first access concentration and then the concentration of attainment of 'boundless space'. Thus he enters upon the first formless base (which is the fifth in the overall series of absorptions).

With the complete surmounting of perceptions of matter, with the disappearance of perceptions of sense-reaction, and no attention given to perceptions of variety, [aware of] 'boundless space', he enters upon and dwells in the base consisting of boundless space.[121]

2.3.2 *Sixth Absorption: Second Formless Base (Boundless Consciousness)*

Once the first formless base has been well developed, the meditator, on emerging from it, reviews it in the usual manner and considers its flaws, in the sense that it suffers from the proximity of the preceding absorption (i.e. the fourth formal absorption) and that it is not as peaceful as the next higher absorption, which has 'boundless consciousness' as its base. Then, turning away from the contemplation of space (boundless space), he proceeds to the contemplation of the state of consciousness itself which had arisen with space as its base. This is a process of becoming aware of awareness, in which the meditator takes as his subject 'the consciousness that occurred pervading that space [i.e. that of the first formless base], adverting again and again as "consciousness, consciousness".'[122] Persevering in this way, the meditator achieves successively access concentration and the concentration of attainment of 'boundless consciousness': 'By completely surmounting the base consisting of boundless space, [aware of] "boundless consciousness", he enters upon and dwells in the base consisting of boundless consciousness.'[123]

2.3.3 *Seventh Absorption: Third Formless Base (Nothingness)*[124]

The progressive discarding of factors reaches here a very high degree of abstraction. The material object (*kasiṇa*) had been discarded in order to contemplate the space it occupied (consciousness of space); the space was discarded to concentrate exclusively on the state of awareness based on it, i.e. to contemplate the act of awareness itself (consciousness of consciousness); now consciousness is left behind, to contemplate what remains when everything has been removed, that is to say, nothing (consciousness of nothingness).

This, of course, is more easily said than done or even conceived. In fact, we are quite used, intellectually, to handling the mathematical and philosophical concepts of 'zero' and 'nothing'. Experientially, however, we do *not* know what it is to 'experience nothingness'. Nor can we come to know it, except by practising this seventh absorption (or similar exercises which give access to the same experience in other meditative traditions). The *Visuddhi Magga* does its best to give an idea, with one of its typically picturesque images:

Suppose a man sees a community of monks gathered together in a meeting hall, or some such place, and then goes away. Then, after the monks have risen at the conclusion of the business for which they had met, and have departed, the man comes back, and as he stands in the doorway looking at that place again, he sees it only as void, he sees it only as secluded, he does not think 'so many monks [of those that were originally present] have died, so many have left the district', but rather he sees only the non-existence thus: 'this is void, secluded'; so too, having formerly dwelt seeing – with the eye of the absorption belonging to the base of boundless consciousness – the consciousness that had occurred with the space as its object, now when that consciousness has disappeared owing to his giving attention . . . in the way beginning: 'there is not, there is not', he dwells seeing only its non-existence, in other words its departedness.[125]

The procedure for moving on to this next stage is always the same: on emerging from the sixth absorption, the meditator considers its flaws and sees that it suffers from the proximity of the fifth absorption (boundless space), which is less subtle, and that it is itself less peaceful than the seventh absorption, based on nothingness. Then the meditator 'should give his attention to the non-existence, voidness and secluded aspect' resulting from the cessation of the consciousness of space (which was itself the subject for the contemplation of the 'consciousness of consciousness' which is the sixth absorption). With this voidness and nonexistence as the subject, the meditator 'adverts again and again in this way: "there is not, there is not" or "void, void" or "secluded, secluded".' Persevering in this manner, he achieves access concentration and then the concentration of attainment of nothingness, and with it the seventh absorption (third formless base): 'by completely surmounting the base consisting of boundless consciousness, [aware that] "there is nothing'', he enters upon and dwells in the base consisting of nothingness.'[126]

2.3.4 *Eighth Absorption: Fourth Formless Base (neither Perception nor Non-Perception)*

If the seventh absorption was already difficult to conceive, how much more so this last one, which represents an altered state of consciousness that cannot be grasped, however one may try, by means of logical discourse. In strict logic, how can a state be understood which involves, simultaneously, the absence of both perception and non-perception? At this stage all that can be said is that such things have to be experienced for oneself, that great perseverance is required, and that the guidance of an experienced master is essential.

To complete this overview, however, let us see the corresponding section of the *Visuddhi Magga* on the procedure to be followed, which is always similar to that of the previous stages. Here again the basic step consists in leaving behind the state that has been attained and to move on to an even more abstract one:

Then he should see the danger in the base consisting of nothingness, and the advantage in what is superior to it, in this way: 'This attainment has the base consisting of boundless consciousness as its near enemy, and it is not as peaceful as the base consisting of neither perception nor non-perception', or in this way: 'Perception is a disease, perception is a boil, perception is a dart, . . . this is peaceful, this is sublime, that is to say neither perception nor non-perception.'[127] So having ended his attachment to the base consisting of nothingness, he should give attention to the base consisting of neither perception nor non-perception, as peaceful. He should advert again and again to that attainment of the base consisting of nothingness that has occurred making non-existence its object, adverting to it as: 'peaceful, peaceful'. . . . As he directs his mind again and again on to that sign[128] in this way, the hindrances[129] are suppressed, mindfulness is established, and his mind becomes concentrated in access. He cultivates that sign again and again, develops and repeatedly practises it. As he does so, consciousness belonging to the base consisting of neither perception nor non-perception arises in absorption.[130]

Thus the meditator attains the eighth absorption (fourth formless base), which is defined as follows: 'By completely surmounting the base consisting of nothingness, he enters upon and dwells in the base consisting of neither perception nor non-perception.'[131]

2.4 *Note on the Attainment of Cessation (*nirodha samāpatti)

In the practice of pure tranquillity meditation the eighth absorption is the highest level of attainment. There is, beyond this, a very uncommon state which can be attained only by a meditator who has fully mastered not only all the stages of tranquillity but also the practice of insight (which will be the subject of the next chapter). This is a state of supreme absorption, in which physiological functions are almost entirely suspended, and is known as the 'cessation of perception and sensation' (*saññā vedayita nirodha*) or the 'attainment of cessation' (*nirodha samāpatti*).

To attain this state it is essential both to have mastered all the eight absorptions of tranquillity meditation and also to have reached one of the last two levels of insight meditation (i.e. 'non-return' or 'holiness' – see chapter 6, section 2.6.1). Obviously, such full mastery of both disciplines (tranquillity and insight) is extremely rare. Moreover, the practice of the absorptions as such, even at the most advanced levels, is of no great interest to someone who, through insight, has attained, or is close to attaining, the fullness of *nibbāna*. Such a one has already left far behind, as if they were childhood games, all concerns with particular states of consciousness or beatific experiences – no matter how satisfactory – unless there is a functional justification for them in specific circumstances. (The Buddha, for instance, resorted to entering upon and dwelling in the absorptions in order to control ill health and physical pain during the last months of his life, so as to be able to complete the final journey he had set himself.) Nevertheless, this presentation would not be complete without some brief account of the attainment of cessation and for this purpose we turn once again to the *Visuddhi Magga*.[132]

As a preliminary, the meditator should go through all the stages of absorption up to the seventh, and should in each case exercise the 'two powers', that is to say, the 'power of tranquillity' to enter upon and dwell in each absorption and the 'power of insight' in reviewing each one of them, in order to see and experience fully the impermanence, lack of essence (i.e. non-self) and consequent unsatisfactoriness of even such subtle and serene experiences.

On emerging from the seventh absorption, the meditator intending to reach attainment of cessation prepares himself mentally in certain ways, including, among other points, deciding in advance how long he will remain in the state of cessation (something like mentally 'setting the alarm'). Then he enters upon the eighth absorption and goes directly from this into cessation. While he is in the state of cessation (which may not last beyond a maximum of seven days), the suspension of vital functions is so complete that the meditator appears to be dead. The difference, of course, lies in the fact that the cessation is a temporary, and not a definitive, one. As it is said in one of the canonical discourses, in which Sāriputta, one of the two leading disciples of the Buddha, instructs another monk, the difference is that

when a monk is dead, he has completed his term, his bodily, verbal and mental formations have ceased and are quite still, his life is exhausted, his heat has subsided, and his faculties are broken up. When a monk, however, has entered upon the cessation of perception and sensation, his bodily, verbal and mental formations also have ceased and are quite still, but his life is unexhausted, his heat has not subsided, and his faculties are quite whole.[133]

3 Conclusion

In closing this brief discussion of Buddhist tranquillity meditation, it is worth recalling the point made at the beginning of chapter 3: this is an abstractive kind of meditation, which is not essentially different from the techniques used in other meditative traditions (especially in Hinduism, but also in other cultures; Kabbalah and Sufi meditations are also of this type[134]).

These were the techniques (except, of course, for the attainment of cessation) to which Gotama the prince turned after abandoning his royal home. He tried them out and found them incapable of producing the definitive enlightenment he sought. In modern terms we might say that he found that they produced altered *states* of consciousness, but did not result in a definitive transmutation of consciousness with its own characteristic *traits*. This is why he left the two great Yoga teachers with whom he had been practising and struck out on his own. The result of his endeavours was *vipassanā*, insight meditation, which, as I said before (chapter 3), is the distinctively Buddhist meditation. The next two chapters are devoted to its practice and ultimate results.

6
Vipassanā – *Development of Insight*

1 All meditation practice, as has been stressed all along, begins by concentrating the mind. For the development of insight – *vipassanā* meditation – it will be recalled that it is enough to achieve access, or momentary, concentration without attempting the higher degree of fixed, or attainment, concentration.[135] The latter is, of course, essential for the development of tranquillity. The abstractive nature of the states of absorption attained in tranquillity practice, however, is not suitable for the development of insight. In fact, what is needed for the purpose of insight, as has been pointed out,[136] is precisely the opposite of abstraction; it is not an increasingly radical turning away from sensory and mental inputs, but rather the unbroken and mindful awareness – within the area selected for attention – of all such inputs as they arise, in order to discern – through a direct experiencing, free from distortions or delusions – their true nature. The choice of meditation subject is therefore particularly important, so as to ensure that it is well suited to the practice of mindfulness unclouded by mental constructs.

Over half of the forty basic meditation subjects (twenty-six to be precise) are not suitable for *vipassanā* practice, either because they are of the reflective type – such as eight of the ten recollections[137] and the four sublime states[138] – or because they involve the abstractive approach, which (by excluding all phenomena and eventually even the initial subject itself) does not allow for the open receptiveness which is essential for *vipassanā*. This is the case with the ten *kasiṇas*[139] or, even more so, with the four immaterial states.[140]

Of the remaining fourteen subjects, two have already been mentioned as especially suitable for the practice of *vipassanā*: mindfulness of the body and mindfulness of breathing.[141] To these may be added the analysis of the four elements[142] and the ten kinds of body decay[143] as well as the perception of the repulsiveness of food.[144]

In spite of the traditional grouping under different headings, these various exercises can be seen at once to be all related in some way to the contemplation of the body from various points of view, for example, the body's functioning (breathing, postures, movements, activities), its parts, the substances and processes of nutrition, the basic elements of which it is composed, and the dead body in various stages of decay.

This focusing on the body is far from accidental. It cannot be sufficiently emphasized that the practice of *vipassanā* consists in the painstaking observation of the world of phenomena, i.e. in paying precise and penetrating attention to whatever is happening *as it is happening* – and what better field of observation than this organism of ours, always present, always available, and which is at one and the same time the object and the subject of the process of perception, experimenter and experiment, the seer and the seen?

In the ultimate analysis, our only source of information, our only working tool for coming to grips with the universe is, precisely, our total organism – the body with its five senses and the mind which operates in and through it. This is why the Buddha said: 'It is in this very fathom-long body, with its perceptions and with its mind, that I make known the world, and the arising of the world, and the extinction of the world, and the path leading to the extinction of the world.'[145]

Hence, in the Buddha's teaching, insight meditation exercises are centred on the body: beginning with the most obvious bodily perceptions and moving on, through the mindful observation of all kinds of sensory and mental processes, to comprehend both the physical and the mental aspects of the total organism, to achieve the liberating insight into the radically impermanent and impersonal nature of the processes that make up what we think of ordinarily as our 'self' and the world of this self's desires.

2 The Foundations of Mindfulness (satipaṭṭhāna)

2.1 The Buddha's systematic instructions to his disciples for the practice of *vipassanā* are found in the *Discourse on the Foundations of Mindfulness* (*Satipaṭṭhāna Sutta*), which has been preserved in two virtually identical texts: the tenth discourse in the *Collection of Middle-Length Discourses* (*Majjhima Nikāya*), and the twenty-second in the *Collection of Long Discourses* (*Dīgha Nikāya*).[146] The latter reproduces the exact text of the

75

former, but with an additional section which contains a detailed exposition of the Four Noble Truths. There are excellent translations of both discourses into English,[147] to which the reader can turn to read them in full. For present purposes I shall use extracts from the *Collection of Middle-Length Discourses* (*M.*10) as required for analysis and discussion, but without reproducing it in its entirety.

The *Discourse on the Foundations of Mindfulness* is one of the most famous of all the Buddha's discourses, and rightly so, since it constitutes the primary source for the practice of insight meditation as taught by the Buddha himself. The measured solemnity of the opening words clearly shows the importance which he attached to the instruction dispensed therein:

This is the only way, monks, for the purification of beings, for the overcoming of sorrow and lamentation, for the destroying of pain and grief, for reaching the right path, for the realization of *Nibbāna*, namely the four Foundations of Mindfulness.[148]

The discourse explains the exercise of mindfulness in relation to four areas of attention which together comprise the whole range of processes that make up the total organism (body and mind). Insight is developed and perfected through the mindful, non-reactive observation of physical and mental processes and events (the right mindfulness factor of the Noble Eightfold Path) as they occur.

Immediately after the opening words just quoted, the Buddha defines the four Foundations of Mindfulness, as follows:

contemplation of the body,

contemplation of sensations,

contemplation of the mind (mental states), and

contemplation of mental objects (mental contents).

The practice of mindfulness on these four foundations is then described in individual sections, one for each exercise, but before that the Buddha makes a point of carefully defining *how* mindfulness is to be practised for the purpose of insight:

Herein, monks, a monk[149] dwells contemplating the body in the body, ardent, clearly comprehending and mindful, having overcome covetousness and grief concerning the world; he dwells contemplating the sensations in the sensations . . . , the mind in the mind . . . , mental objects in mental objects, ardent, clearly comprehending and mindful, having overcome covetousness and grief concerning the world.

The repeated reference to 'contemplating the body *in the body*. . . , the sensations *in the sensations* . . . ,' etc., may seem somewhat odd at first, but its proper understanding is essential for correct practice. The point of this particular phrasing is to stress that what has to be practised is *pure, non-reactive mindfulness*, i.e. as clear and full an awareness as possible of whatever is present *now* in the area selected for observation, without immediately going off at a tangent – as the unconcentrated mind tends to do – into other more or less relevant mental associations (thoughts, feelings, value judgements, imaginings). Two quotations from other discourses of the Buddha make this extremely clear:

Fare along contemplating the body in the body, but do not apply yourself to a train of thought connected with the body; fare along contemplating the sensations in the sensations . . . , the mind in the mind . . . , mental objects in mental objects, but do not apply yourself to a train of thought connected with sensations . . . , the mind . . . , mental objects.[150]

Thus must you train yourself: 'In the seen there will be just the seen; in the heard, just the heard; in the sensed, just the sensed; in the cognized, just the cognized. That is how you must train yourself.[151]

The reason is obvious enough: the moment you start indulging in thoughts, feelings, etc., *about* the observation you are no longer *observing*. It is this constant shift *away* from what is actually there that the exercise is designed to correct.

Let us now return to the discourse and consider each one of the four Foundations of Mindfulness, in the order in which they appear in it.

2.2 *Contemplation of the Body (* kāyānupassanā)

As already mentioned in chapter 4, on concentration, there are different kinds of body-contemplation exercises, which may be suitable at various times and for different purposes, depending on circumstances and on the character and disposition of the meditator.[152] One of them, however, is of fundamental importance and universal application, suitable at all times and for everyone. This is the mindfulness of breathing (*ānāpānasati*), which the Buddha recommended most particularly for the practice of *vipassanā* and which, it will be recalled, was the method he himself used on the occasion of his definitive Enlightenment.[153]

Mindfulness of breathing is not only an excellent means of concentrating the mind in order to proceed with *vipassanā* or *samatha* practice, but it is also a complete exercise in itself which, 'developed and repeatedly practised' – as the Buddha stressed – leads to the highest attainments. It is therefore not surprising that the discussion of body contemplation as one of the Foundations of Mindfulness should begin with mindfulness of breathing.

2.2.1 *Mindfulness of Breathing*

2.2.1.1 *General Instructions*

First, the physical and mental preparation:

And how, monks, does a monk dwell contemplating the body in the body? Herein, monks, a monk, having gone to the forest, to the foot of a tree, or to an empty place, sits down crosslegged, keeps his body erect and establishes mindfulness about the mouth.

The crosslegged posture (in lotus or half-lotus), with the body erect and the hands resting palms upward in the meditator's lap – as portrayed in innumerable images – is, of course, the traditional meditative posture. There are excellent reasons for adopting it, as it is a very stable position, which (provided that the spine is kept straight, but not tense, and well balanced on the pelvis) can be maintained comfortably for very long periods, and also because the calm and collected body posture helps to induce a calm and collected state of mind. However, if one has difficulty with it, any comfortable seated position may be adopted. The important thing is to be able to remain motionless, alert but not tense, for a good length of time.[154]

The instruction concerning the establishing of mindfulness 'about the mouth' has been translated literally above, exactly as it is found in the original discourse in Pali. This is a phrase which has often caused difficulties to scholars and translators who – having no practical experience of the exercise – did not see the point of the literal phrase, thought it should be read as establishing or arousing 'mindfulness in front [of oneself]'[155] and interpreted it as a metaphor for 'fixing the attention by directing it towards the breath, which is in front' or, more briefly, as keeping one's 'mindfulness alert'.[156] For someone with practical experience of the exercise, however, the literal phrase is perfectly clear. As the well-known contemporary *vipassanā* master S. N. Goenka explains,[157] 'about the mouth' indicates that the area to which attention must be directed for the mindful contemplation of the breath includes not only the tip of the nose (which is the obvious spot), but also the upper lip just below the nostrils, which is where one may most easily perceive the touch sensation of the breath going in and coming out of the nostrils.

Once comfortably installed, the meditator begins the mindful contemplation of breathing.

Mindful he breathes in, and mindful he breathes out. Breathing in a long breath, he knows 'I breathe in a long breath'; breathing out a long breath, he knows 'I breathe out a long breath.' Breathing in a short breath, he knows 'I breathe in a short breath'; breathing out a short breath, he knows 'I breathe out a short breath.' 'Experiencing the whole body, I shall breathe in,' thus he trains himself; 'Experiencing the whole body I shall breathe out,' thus he trains himself. 'Calming bodily processes, I shall breathe in,' thus he trains himself; 'Calming bodily processes, I shall breathe out,' thus he trains himself.

Note that the exercise falls into three parts, each one of which comprises the complete breathing-in/breathing-out cycle:

1. *Awareness of the act of breathing as such*, including both long and short in-breaths and out-breaths;

2. *Awareness of the body while breathing*: 'Experiencing the whole body, I shall breathe in/breathe out . . .';

3. *Calming of bodily processes while breathing*: 'Calming bodily processes, I shall breathe in/breathe out . . .'.

Let us take them one by one.

2.2.1.2 *Awareness of Breathing*

This is developed by concentrating one's attention on the area just mentioned (which was already referred to in chapter 4, section 4.3.10), that is to say, on the nostrils and the upper lip just below them. It is essential *not* to attempt any kind of breath control (unlike in certain Yoga exercises), but simply to let the breath come naturally, sometimes slower and deeper (long in-breath/out-breath), sometimes shallower and faster (short in-breath/out-breath). The meditator must do nothing but pay the closest possible attention to the contact of the ingoing and outcoming airflow with any point or points in the area of observation, staying strictly within it and disregarding any other points connected with the action of breathing (such as the throat, chest or diaphragm). It is also very important to follow each in-breath and out-breath uninterruptedly from beginning to end, with full awareness of its duration, intensity, location and the character of the touch sensations it generates.

2.2.1.3 *Awareness of the Body while Breathing*

In this instruction and also in the following one, 'body' may be understood in two ways. According to the old commentaries, 'body', in this context, means 'the whole body of air involved in a complete in-breath or out-breath'. The *Visuddhi Magga*, for instance, following the commentaries, says:

> He trains thus: 'I shall breathe in . . . , I shall breathe out making known, making plain, the beginning, middle and end of the entire in-breath body . . . , out-breath body.' Making them known, making them plain in this way, he both breathes in and breathes out with consciousness associated with knowledge. That is why it is said: 'He trains thus: "I shall breathe in . . . , I shall breathe out experiencing the whole body." '[158]

Therefore, according to this tradition of textual interpretation (which has also been followed by certain modern authors[159]), 'experiencing the whole body' refers to the mindful, deliberate experiencing of each whole breath, and thus this second instruction simply reinforces the first by stressing the importance of mindfully following the course of each breath in its entirety.

This is unexceptionable as far as it goes but, in the light of practical experience, it does not do justice to the full import of the instruction. According to the empirical tradition, especially as preserved in Burma (a country which, together with Sri Lanka and Thailand, is the repository of the oldest traditions of the Buddha's teaching),[160] the requirement to train 'experiencing the whole body' should be taken literally, and refers to what is, in fact, a further stage in the practice. Here, the mindfulness developed by devoting concentrated attention to the in-breaths and out-breaths is now applied to the contemplation of other processes and phenomena which are constantly taking place in one's body, or rather, to put it more accurately, to the contemplation of the interplay of multiple phenomena which, at the physical level, constitute what we call 'body' in common parlance. This is the typical *vipassanā* exercise, the concrete practice for the development of insight. Further details about its contemporary practice will be found in chapter 9.[161]

2.2.1.4 *Calming of Bodily Processes while Breathing*

Here, too, there are two interpretations. According to the textual tradition, 'calming bodily processes' means 'calming the bodily function (of breathing)'. This is how it is translated in the influential modern manual *The Heart of Buddhist Meditation*, with the explanation that 'implicit in that observation there will be the wish and effort to bring still greater calmness to the respiratory and mental process involved.'[162] Seen thus, this is rather a *samatha* exercise, conducive to the development of tranquillity.

According to the empirical tradition, on the other hand, what is involved is the calming not only of the respiratory (and related mental) process, but of bodily processes generally. Moreover, the calming is the result of the wish and effort, not to achieve calmness as such, but to develop mindfulness. The calming of bodily processes is something that occurs naturally when they are subjected to mindful, non-reactive contemplation. In fact, the close, mindful inspection of these processes sharpens the meditator's awareness, and he becomes increasingly conscious of processes and events which are normally subliminal, i.e. below the threshold of conscious perception of the unconcentrated mind. It is a fact of experience that the progressive conscious grasp of ever subtler processes has a calming effect both on the mind (observing process) and on the body (observed process). In this view, therefore, this is a further stage of *vipassanā*, in which insight is developed and deepened through the direct, undistracted contemplation of the body, and the calming is, as it were, a by-product.

2.2.1.5 *Compendium of Practice*

The first section on the contemplation of the body ends with a passage (which is also repeated at the end of all the other sections) that needs to be examined very carefully, because it sums up the essence of the exercises and of the mental attitude necessary for successful practice:

He dwells contemplating the body in the body internally, or externally, or both internally and externally. He dwells contemplating the arising of phenomena in the body, or contemplating the passing away of phenomena in the body, or the arising and passing away of phenomena in the body. Or the mindfulness that 'there is a body' is established in him to the extent necessary for knowledge and mindfulness. He dwells independent, clinging to nothing in the world. Thus, indeed, monks, a monk dwells contemplating the body in the body.

The reference to contemplating the body 'internally, or externally, or both internally and externally' has also been the subject of varying interpretations. The text says, quite literally, 'internally' and 'externally'.[163] In the empirical tradition, this is understood as an explanation of the specific method used to develop mindfulness with the whole body as its subject. In fact, in *vipassanā* practice the meditator scans the body methodically, with concentrated attention, without neglecting any part of it, to become aware of whatever sensations occur from moment to moment. This scanning takes place to begin with on the surface of the body (to observe surface sensations) and is then also carried out in depth (i.e. inside the mass of the body, to observe internal sensations). Both variants are then practised from time to time, alternating surface scanning ('externally', since it is on the outside of the body) and in-depth scanning ('internally'). As the meditator's skill develops, improving the clarity and fineness of perception, the exercise of whole-body awareness may be practised, which involves the simultaneous perception of surface and depth sensations ('both internally and externally').

The textual tradition, on the other hand, following the old commentaries, maintains that 'internally' refers to the contemplation of one's own breathing, and 'externally' to the contemplation of someone else's breathing: 'According to that first part of the "Instructions", each single exercise has to be applied first to oneself, then to others (in general or to a definite person just observed) and finally to both.'[164]

In actual fact, the two views need not be regarded as contradictory, but rather as complementary, in the sense that both are practicable and useful for the development of insight. The basic exercise, of course, is the one carried out on one's own organism: to develop the mindful, clear comprehension of phenomena in oneself, both on the surface and in depth. It is a fact, however, that when the fineness of perception has been sufficiently developed, the practitioner is able to perceive the arising and passing away of phenomena not only in himself but also in others. He can 'tune in', as it were, to what is going on in them.

A supplementary interpretation has recently been propounded by the Spanish orientalist Professor Ramiro A. Calle.[165] This, although rather more speculative in approach, makes – I believe – a useful contribution to our conceptual understanding of the processes involved. According to this view, 'internally' and 'externally' may be taken to denote different experiential levels of meditative practice. When contemplating 'internally', the meditator is still close to the *subjective* attitude typical of everyday experience. He feels that: '*I* am contemplating the body' (or, later on, the sensations, the mind, etc.). As the process of getting away from this delusional 'I' conception progresses, *objective* contemplation is achieved. That is to say that the perceptual act is no longer identified with a perceiving 'I', but is experienced 'externally', as a perceiving process which has as its object a perceived process (body, sensations, etc.). Finally even this perceptual act/percept duality disappears: 'both internally and externally' denotes then the simultaneous aspects of a single contemplative experience, which no longer involves a subject/object distinction.

To come back to the passage under discussion: after telling us *how* to contemplate, the instructions specify *what* is, in fact, contemplated, and this is very important. It is the *arising* and the *passing away* of phenomena.

That is to say that the purpose is to develop the fullest and sharpest possible awareness of the unceasing fluctuation of the phenomena observed, which reveals their unstable and impermanent nature: 'Transient are all the elements of being.'[166] Each moment of what we think of as 'our' existence, 'our' life, is a swirl of instantaneous events, continually arising and passing away. At the physical level, which is the one with which we are concerned at this moment, it is a well-known fact that millions of the cells that make up the living tissue of our bodies decay or are destroyed every day, and are replaced by new, equally transient, ones, so that at every instant there are literally millions of 'deaths' and 'births' occurring in our bodies, and none of the cellular components of the present fabric were there a few years ago, or will be there a few years (or, in some cases, a few moments) hence. This at the physical level. But at the mental level, too, how many more or less clearly formulated thoughts flash through our minds every moment? How many times a day do our intentions, expectations and states of mind fluctuate and change, not infrequently with staggering rapidity?

The meditator, then, through close observation of the body, experiences the arising and passing away of phenomena and establishes the awareness that 'there is a body' *to the extent necessary for knowledge and mindfulness*. Now, what is the precise meaning of this last phrase? Simply that the conscious experiencing of the multiple processes that we call 'body' is developed for the exclusive purpose of mindful contemplation, without allowing oneself to be tempted into any kind of reflection, speculation, imagination, desires, hopes, fears or any other mental constructs or emotional impulses related to this 'body', its identity, durability, past or future, its hypothetical relationship with a soul, self or personality, etc. This is what is meant by 'contemplating the body in the body'. And the knowledge thus attained is the comprehension through direct experience of the unstable and impermanent nature of the phenomena of which it is composed. As the Venerable Nyānaponika says:

. . . 'The body exists', 'feeling exists', etc., but no separate self, no abiding personality or soul. These words of the text indicate the results in terms of insight, i.e. the realistic view of things as they actually are.[167]

I have dwelt at some length on the exact phrasing of this passage because of its great importance as a compendium of the purpose and meaning of the practice of the Foundations of Mindfulness. This is made very clear in the discourse itself by the fact that the compendium is repeated in its entirety not only at the end of each one of the body-contemplation exercises, but also in the sectibns on the other three

Foundations of Mindfulness (only with the necessary changes to introduce the appropriate references to 'sensations', 'mind' and 'mental
objects'). Naturally enough, since it is the nature of *all* phenomena –
whether physical or mental – to be impermanent, and what is sought is,
precisely, full insight into this fact.

To proceed with the analysis of the discourse. As has been repeatedly
pointed out, the mindfulness of breathing exercise is the most essential
one and is most generally used for the purpose of insight. This is why it
comes first in the discourse and why I have spent more time on it than
will be devoted to the remaining body-contemplation exercises to which
the discourse now turns. It must be stressed, however, that these other
exercises are also highly effective and beneficial, either for use in conjunction with the mindfulness of breathing, or as alternatives to it, depending on the person and circumstances.[168]

2.2.2 *Awareness of Body Postures and Movements*

And again, monks, a monk when going, knows 'I am going'; when standing,
he knows 'I am standing'; when sitting, he knows 'I am sitting'; when lying
down, he knows 'I am lying down.' Whatever position the body is in, he
knows it.

The point here, as in all these exercises, is to achieve full awareness of
every action or experience as it is occurring, and not, as is usually the
case, doing something more or less automatically while thinking or half
thinking about various other things. Nothing should happen 'automatically', nothing should go by unnoticed. Unflagging mindfulness
must be maintained. In this exercise mindfulness is directed at the basic
postures of the body and at the action of walking, which are, of course,
amongst the most common and unreflectingly performed activities of
our daily life.

2.2.2.1 *As Main Exercise*

As the main exercise, this consists in observing with scrupulous attention the changing positions of the body, its movements and the accompanying sensations (from the most obvious to the most subtle) which are
continually arising and passing away throughout the organism. The
procedure is similar to that of 'experiencing the whole body' while
breathing in the previous exercise,[169] but with the difference that, in this
case, one does not start from the breathing but proceeds directly to the
observation of the body.

2.2.2.2 *Walking Meditation (*cankamana*)*

Mindful walking is frequently used as a main exercise in *vipassanā* meditation (and also very often alternating with periods of sitting meditation – see section 2.2.2.3 below). In Buddhist monasteries or meditation centres, especially in Southeast Asia, 'meditation walks' or 'meditation terraces' are often to be found, specifically laid out for the purpose of walking meditation (*cankamana*). These walks are straight, level and even, so that the meditator is not distracted by changes of direction or irregularities of the surface as he walks back and forth, concentrating on the walking movement. The meditation walk should not be too short (not less than some twenty paces as a minimum), as turning round too frequently can be distracting; but it should not be too long because, especially for a beginner, it is difficult to maintain mindfulness during too long a stretch. The normal length is some thirty to forty paces, although some walks may exceptionally go up to as much as sixty.

There are different schools of thought as regards the manner of walking. Some masters teach a very slow walk, breaking up each step into as many as six stages (lifting the foot – moving it forward – farther forward – lowering it – touching the ground – taking the weight); others use three subdivisions (lifting – forward – lowering and putting down), the rhythm being correspondingly less slow; others still use only two subdivisions (lifting and forward – lowering and putting down). Finally, there are masters who recommend moving at a speed which, although measured, approximates that of a normal, unhurried walk, pointing out that in this way it is easier to learn to apply mindfulness while walking in everyday life, i.e. outside formal meditation periods. These same masters also allow rather more latitude as regards the phases of the movement that should be particularly noticed, leaving it to the student himself to discover which are the aspects to which his attention turns more naturally.

Some notice the contact of the feet on the earth, others the movements of the legs, and so on. At first, just be generally mindful of the whole walking process, later the mind will single out something interesting which should be investigated.[170]

Whatever the details of the method used, the basic procedure consists always in walking back and forth along the whole length of the meditation walk, stopping for a moment at each end to check the mind's concentration before turning round. The hands are normally clasped in front of the body, and the eyes cast down, looking at the ground not more than four or five feet ahead.[171] The purpose of the exercise is always the same: mindful observation of bodily processes and phenomena, so as to perceive their continual fluctuations with increasing clarity and penetration.

2.2.2.3 *As Subsidiary Exercise*

Walking meditation is sometimes used as a subsidiary exercise in intensive meditation courses (where participants spend up to fifteen or twenty hours a day meditating), alternating with sessions of sitting meditation devoted to mindfulness of breathing or mindfulness of the body generally. This makes it possible to introduce some variation and to allow for some physical exercise without a break in the continuity of mindfulness.

Mindfulness of the different body postures (standing, sitting, lying down) can also be used as a subsidiary exercise, alternating with whatever main exercise has been selected (most commonly, mindfulness of breathing or else one of the other body-contemplation exercises), always with the purpose of allowing for some variety without interrupting the continuity of mindfulness.

But, of course, mindfulness is not something that should be exercised only in formal meditation training. It should, on the contrary, increasingly permeate one's whole existence. It is therefore always recommended that, as one goes about one's daily business, one should be as mindful as possible of the body's postures and movements, to the extent compatible with the degree of specific concentration required by the task in hand. Clearly, when one is engaged in some demanding intellectual activity (mathematical, verbal-logical, etc.), mindfulness of the body will have to take second place for the duration. Even then, however, one can learn to maintain awareness, for instance of the touch sensations of one's buttocks on the chair, one's feet on the ground or the pen between one's fingers, while working out a mathematical formula or writing an essay. The maintenance of a generalized level of mindfulness during everyday activities, apart from its immediate benefits in terms of alertness, makes it easier for the practitioner, when the moment comes for formal practice, to return to it smoothly and efficiently, and improves the quality of the practice.

2.2.3 *Clear Comprehension of Every Action*[172]

This exercise is an expansion of the one that has just been described:

And again, monks, a monk in going forward and in going back exercises clear comprehension; in looking straight on and in looking elsewhere . . . , in bending and in stretching . . . , in wearing the robes and carrying the almsbowl[173] . . . , in eating, drinking, chewing and savouring . . . , in defecating and in urinating . . . , in walking, standing, sitting, sleeping, waking, in speaking and in keeping silent, he exercises clear comprehension.

As can be seen, this exercise involves paying deliberate attention not only to body postures and movements but also to the routine acts of everyday living, such as eating, drinking, relieving oneself, going out to get one's food (whether this is done by taking up an almsbowl to go begging or a shopping bag to go shopping is, from this point of view, immaterial), going to sleep at night, waking up in the morning, and all the other innumerable things we do every day without paying any special attention to them. In addition to broadening the scope for mindfulness, this exercise introduces a further element, described as 'clear comprehension'. This is the complement, at the intellectual level, of the mindful observation at the perceptual level. When meditation is carried out as an exclusive occupation in a motionless posture, whether seated, standing or lying down, it is, in fact, possible to exercise pure perceptual mindfulness. This is also possible – to all practical purposes – in the course of a period of formal walking meditation. But this is no longer the case when more complex activities are concerned, involving not only a variety of perceptual and motor acts but also elements of intention, judgement, decision making, etc. Think, for instance, of all that is involved in the simple act of putting a morsel of food in one's mouth; picking up fork and knife, cutting the morsel, bringing it up to one's mouth, opening the mouth, introducing the morsel, etc. The performance of even the simplest task necessarily involves the will and the intellect (the task has to be identified, the appropriate means for its performance have to be selected, then comes the carrying out of the various stages of the task, verifying that the desired result has been achieved, and so on). By devoting to these mental components the same kind of deliberate attention as was paid to the bare sense data in the exercises just described, a clear comprehension is developed of the purpose of every action, of the best way of achieving that purpose – both as regards means and their application – and of the exact nature of each act. One can now more easily appreciate why the initial instructions concerning the practice (section 2.1 of this chapter) specify that the meditator dwells 'ardent' (that is to say, practising with all necessary enthusiasm and application), 'clearly comprehending and mindful'.

2.2.4 *Repulsiveness of the Body – The Four Elements – Cemetery Contemplations*

The discourse goes on with three variants of body contemplation which have already been mentioned in chapter 4, on concentration. In the light of what was said there,[174] there is no need to discuss them further now, except to recall that, apart from their usefulness as subjects for concentration, these exercises are particularly suited to counteract excessive attachment to physical appearance and sensual enjoyment, since they focus attention on the most striking aspects of the precarious and often enough even repulsive character of body processes and functions, and on the thoroughly impersonal nature of the elements that make up the organism. As in the preceding sections, each one of these three exercises, which complete the range of body-contemplation practices described in the discourse, closes with the summary compendium of practice, recalling that the meditator always

dwells contemplating the body in the body internally, or externally, or both internally and externally. He dwells contemplating the arising . . . , the passing away . . . , or the arising and passing away of phenomena in the body. Or the mindfulness that 'there is a body' is established in him to the extent necessary for knowledge and mindfulness.

2.3 *Contemplation of Sensations (vedanānupassanā)*

And how, monks, does a monk dwell contemplating sensations in the sensations? Here, when experiencing a pleasant sensation, the monk knows: 'I experience a pleasant sensation'; when experiencing a painful sensation, he knows: 'I experience a painful sensation'; when experiencing a sensation which is neither pleasant nor painful [i.e. a neutral sensation], he knows: 'I experience a neutral sensation.' When experiencing a pleasant . . . , painful . . . or neutral worldly sensation, he knows: 'I experience a pleasant . . . , painful . . . or neutral worldly sensation'; when experiencing a pleasant . . . , painful . . . or neutral unworldly sensation, he knows: 'I experience a pleasant . . . , painful . . . or neutral unworldly sensation.'

It must be clearly understood that traditional Buddhist psychology identifies six senses in human beings, i.e. the five bodily senses plus the mind. The mind, in fact, in addition to being the faculty which receives and identifies the data supplied by the bodily senses, may well be regarded as one more sense, with its own specific data: it perceives and observes directly (that is to say, without the mediation of the bodily senses) all that happens at the strictly mental and affective level – ideas, volitions, emotions, etc. Therefore, since the mind is considered as one more sense, it must be understood that, in the Buddhist tradition, 'sensations' include the whole range of inputs, both from physical sources (as perceived by the five bodily senses) and from mental sources (perceived directly by the mind), which are identified and evaluated by the discriminative function of the mind itself.

Of course, the contemplation of the body already is, in fact, a contemplation of bodily sensations since, as has just been seen, body contemplation is carried out through the mindful observation of sensations as they occur. The difference lies in the fact that, in the contemplation of the body pure and simple, attention is focused strictly on the recognition or identification of the data without any value judgements. In the specific exercise of contemplation of sensations, on the other hand, the area of observation is broadened to include mental 'sensations' (as just defined), and the subject for contemplation is, precisely, the evaluating activity of the mind.

The process of evaluation, that is to say, the mental classification of a body sensation or of a thought (mental sensation) as 'pleasant', 'painful' or 'neutral', is something which we do all the time, automatically and instantaneously, at every moment of our waking lives (and also in dreams). Normally, we act or, rather, react accordingly in an equally automatic manner – especially at the physical level – to avoid or get rid of whatever is painful or unpleasant, and to obtain or retain whatever is pleasant, while neutral data tend to be regarded with indifference.[175] Now the aim of meditative contemplation, here as in other exercises, is to do away with automatic reactions and develop mindfulness. The meditator focuses attention on the process of evaluation, so as to be fully aware of the quality of the sensation as perceived (pleasant, painful or neutral), i.e. of the precise value judgement that has taken place, *without reacting*. Reaction is always due to desire (*wanting* what seems – i.e. is perceived and evaluated as – good and *not wanting* what seems bad), to attachment arising from an incorrect understanding of the true nature of the experience.[176] Let us again quote from the Venerable Nyānaponika's authoritative handbook:

If, in receiving a sense-impression, one is able to pause and stop at the phase of Feeling [i.e. sensation], and make it, in its very first stage of manifestation, the object of Bare Attention, Feeling will not be able to originate Craving or other passions. It will stop at the bare statements of 'pleasant', 'unpleasant' or 'indifferent', giving Clear Comprehension time to enter and decide about the attitude or action to be taken. Furthermore, if one notices, in Bare Attention, the conditioned arising of feeling [i.e. the arising and passing away of phenomena], one will find from one's own experience that there is no necessity at all for being carried away by passionate reaction, which will start a new concatenation of suffering.[177]

This is how the meditator contemplates 'sensations in the sensations', exactly in the same manner as the body is contemplated in the body, without any kind of additions or elaborations, always exclusively concerned with the exact experiencing of each moment and gaining thus an increasingly clear and full understanding of the impermanent and impersonal nature of all phenomena.

The reference to *worldly* and *unworldly* sensations requires some elucidation. Worldly sensations are those which arise in connection with all the events and experiences of ordinary life – the satisfactions and pleasures, annoyances and pains, or states of mental and physical indifference which we experience every day. Unworldly sensations are those which relate to the efforts, satisfactions and dissatisfactions involved in the pursuit of understanding through meditative development; for instance, the happiness and bliss which arise in the first absorption,[178] the phases of inertia, discouragement or anxiety, or elation and enthusiasm that may sometimes occur, etc.

The section on the contemplation of sensations closes with the important 'Compendium of Practice', which has already been discussed in some detail on its first appearance in connection with mindfulness of breathing (section 2.2.1.5 of this chapter).

2.4 *Contemplation of the Mind* (cittānupassanā)

And how, monks, does a monk dwell contemplating the mind in the mind? Here, a monk knows the mind with greed as greedy; the mind without greed as not greedy; the mind with hate as hating; the mind without hate as not hating; the mind with delusion as deluded; the mind without delusion as undeluded; the shrunken mind as shrunken; the distracted mind as distracted; the developed mind as developed; the undeveloped mind as undeveloped; the surpassable mind as surpassable; the unsurpassable mind as unsurpassable; the concentrated mind as concentrated; the unconcentrated mind as unconcentrated; the freed mind as freed; the mind not freed as not-freed.[179]

In this contemplation attention is directed to mental states. Just as in the contemplation of the body, bodily processes were subjected to mindful, non-reactive scrutiny so as to develop an increasingly penetrating perception of very subtle, normally subliminal, events, the same kind of scrutiny is now applied to mental states. The purpose is to see quite clearly, moment by moment, the exact state and condition of the mind at that particular point in time.

This can be practised as a main exercise for the development of insight. However, it is also very useful as an auxiliary in the contemplation of the body and of sensations. It is, in fact, essential in the early stages of these contemplations, as a means of avoiding breaks in the continuity of conscious, deliberate attention. In fact, while practising the contemplation of the body or of sensations, every time that the mind wanders from the strict concentration on the body or the sensations (i.e. as thoughts, associations of ideas, emotions, etc., arise), the meditator should at once devote full momentary attention to the arising mental state, not in order to pursue it any further but, on the contrary, simply to note it with full awareness, dismiss it, and then immediately go back, quite deliberately, to the contemplation of the body. This 'noting' is a momentary contemplation of the mind and its point is to prevent the break in continuity of attention which would otherwise occur if the mind wandered unnoticed (as so often happens in everyday life, when one suddenly notices that one has for some time been thinking, dreaming or emoting about something more or less unconnected with the matter in hand). By turning the mind wandering, i.e. the arising mental state, into the momentary object of mindful awareness, the integrity of mindfulness is maintained, which consists always in being fully aware of what is there at any given moment.[180]

Apart from its usefulness in formal meditation, contemplation of the mind or mental states also has obvious advantages as a means of developing self-knowledge through calm, dispassionate introspection. Moreover, the habit of immediately 'noting' thoughts, etc., arising during the meditation exercise, once well established, can also be used to considerable advantage in many situations of daily life, in which all too often we tend to react unreflectingly. For instance, the usual angry reaction to someone's unpleasant remark can be neutralized by quickly noting 'angry mind' as the first reaction flares up in oneself. This mindful, detached 'noting', by preventing an unthinking identification with the emotional impulse, helps to maintain mental balance, thus making it possible to respond to the originally perceived aggression in an objectively more adequate manner, which may tend to improve, rather than worsen, the situation.

This section, too, closes with the 'Compendium of Practice', and what was said on this subject in section 2.2.1.5 above is equally valid here, except that, of course, the primary subject of practice now (both in this exercise and in the next one) is the mind and its workings, rather than the body and its sensations. The two are, however, closely interrelated. Thus, the instruction to contemplate 'internally, externally, or both internally and externally' has both mental and physical implications. At the physical level it refers to the awareness of sensations arising in conjunction with mental states, thoughts, etc. (for instance, when mental excitement occurs, one should also be clearly aware of any concurrent speeding up of the heartbeat, or changes in breathing, etc.). At the strictly mental level it should be understood that mental states (or, in the next exercise, mental contents) are, in one way, to be perceived in oneself (internally), in others (externally) and in both simultaneously, and in another way, that they can be experienced at a subjective, an objective and a unified level (which transcends the subject/object distinction).

2.5 *Contemplation of Mental Objects or Mental Contents* (dhammānupassanā)

Mental contents, or the objects of mental activity, are, of course, innumerable. All the subjects of contemplation which have been discussed so far are mental contents to the extent that the mind deals with them: the perceptions of physical processes, the positive, negative or neutral evaluations of sensations, mental states taken as the objects of mindful awareness. To these are now added other categories which are strictly mental in nature, such as the concepts we use in trying to build up a coherent picture of the world, the logical-verbal mechanisms with which we handle the inflow of mental data, the ideals of conduct and knowledge which we develop intellectually, on the basis of our perception of what constitutes reality, and so on.

From this vast field, the Buddha – for the purposes of this discourse – selected five groups which are of particular importance for the development of insight. They are:

(i) the five hindrances;

(ii) the five aggregates of clinging;

(iii) the six senses, with their respective objects (known traditionally as 'the six internal and the six external sense bases'), and the mental fetters which arise in consequence;

(iv) the seven factors of enlightenment;

(v) the Four Noble Truths.

The first and the fourth of these categories[181] belong, in fact, rather to the contemplation of mental states, but they are nevertheless included in this last section of the discourse because, as will be seen, here the exercise goes beyond pure mindful observation and involves deliberate mental activity to eliminate those factors which hinder insight and to promote those which are favourable to its development.

The second and fifth groups belong entirely to the category of mental objects proper, representing different aspects of the Buddhist analysis of reality, always with the specific purpose of developing and perfecting insight. The third group has a dual aspect: on the one hand, it shares the analytical approach in that it deals with the mechanism of sense perception (involving the six 'senses' of Buddhist psychology, i.e. five bodily senses plus the mind) through which we receive and interpret the data of what we call 'reality'; on the other hand, it involves both observing and dealing with mental states, in that it also refers to the consequences of perception in the human psyche (the 'fetters', in traditional terms) which flow from the operation of the perceptual mechanisms.

I should now like to discuss these various factors, not in the order in which they appear in the discourse, but rather – for greater ease of presentation – grouping them into two categories: that of positive and negative mental states – i.e. (i), (iii) and (iv) above – and that of reality analysis – (ii) and (v). The six sense bases and their consequent fetters (iii) are being placed in the first rather than the second category because, for the development of insight, what is most important there is the practical impact at the mental level of perception, i.e. the 'fetters' of the mind.

2.5.1 *Negative and Positive Mental States: Hindrances, Fetters and Factors of Enlightenment*

2.5.1.1 *The Five Hindrances (*nīvaraṇa*)*

Here, monks, a monk dwells contemplating mental objects in the mental objects [that are] the five hindrances. And how does he contemplate? Here, monks, when *sense-desire* is present in him, the monk knows: 'There is sense-desire in me'; or when sense-desire is absent, he knows: 'There is no sense-desire in me.' He knows how the arising of [previously] non-arisen sense-desire comes to be; he knows how the abandoning of arisen sense-desire comes to be; and he knows how the non-arising in the future of the abandoned sense-desire comes to be. When *ill-will* is present in him . . . , when *sloth and torpor* . . . , when *agitation and worry* are present in him . . . , when *doubt* is present in him, the monk knows: 'There is ill-will . . . , sloth and torpor . . . , agitation and worry . . . , doubt in me'; or when ill-will . . . , sloth and torpor . . . , agitation and worry . . . , doubt are absent, he knows: 'There is no ill-will, etc., in me.' He knows how the arising of the [previously] non-arisen ill-will . . . , sloth and torpor . . . , agitation and worry . . . , doubt comes to be; he knows how the abandoning [of these arisen hindrances] comes to be; and he knows how the non-arising in the future [of the abandoned hindrances] comes to be.

The hindrances – sense desire, ill will, sloth and torpor, agitation and worry, and doubt – are so called because they are mental states which, by confusing the mind with desires and hates, by rendering it sluggish or overexcited, make it impossible for it to see and understand things clearly. In another discourse,[182] the Buddha illustrated this with the simile of a pond: if the water is polluted with impurities of different colours (sense desires), if it is all churned up (ill will), if it is choked with weeds and grasses (sloth and torpor), if its surface is ruffled by the wind (agitation and worry), or if it is full of mud (doubt), anyone looking into the pond will not be able to see his own image reflected in the water. Similarly, the mind polluted by the hindrances will not be able to discern what is true and good either for itself or for others.

The first stage of this contemplation consists in the mindful observation of mental contents, so as to be clearly aware of which specific hindrance is arising or is present in the mind at any given moment ('he knows how the arising of non-arisen sense-desire, etc., comes to be'). The second stage (and this is where the difference lies between the exercise of this fourth foundation of mindfulness and the previous three) consists in moving over from pure mindful observation to action: acting with full awareness and clear comprehension of the purpose sought and the best means to achieve it,[183] one now endeavours to overcome and remove, to the extent possible, the hindrance that has been identified ('he knows how the abandoning of arisen sense-desire, etc., comes to be'). I say 'to the extent possible' because, until a very high level of insight has been achieved, all removal or abandonment of the hindrances is only temporary and they reappear again sooner or later; naturally enough since, like all conditioned things, they evidence the 'arising and passing away of phenomena'. This need be no cause for discouragement, provided one always bears in mind that what is essential for the development of insight in this as in all other exercises is to remain alert and equanimous by cultivating the *mindful, non-reactive observation* of whatever is going on. This is, it must be remembered, the point of the instructions contained in the 'Compendium of Practice', repeated so many times in the discourse and again here, as well as at the end of each one of the following sections of the contemplation of the mind:

He dwells contemplating the arising of phenomena in mental objects, or contemplating the passing away of phenomena in mental objects, or the arising and passing away of phenomena in mental objects. Or the mindfulness that 'there are mental objects' is established in him to the extent necessary for knowledge and mindfulness. He dwells independent, clinging to nothing in the world. Thus, indeed, monks, a monk dwells contemplating mental objects in the mental objects [that are] the five hindrances.

Thus, whenever sense desire (or whichever other hindrance) is present in the mind, one notes that 'there is sense desire' (or whatever). As one endeavours to abandon, or turn away from, the existing hindrance, one notes 'endeavour to abandon.' When one has succeeded in so doing, one notes 'absence of sense desire, etc.', noting also whatever sense of satisfaction or achievement may arise on account of the successful endeavour (which is a contemplation of a mental state). When, sooner or later, the hindrance reappears, one again takes note of its presence and perseveres as before.

As one gains experience, one notices that dispassionate observation is, in fact, the best means of disposing of undesirable mental states or contents. Repression or inhibition of negative thoughts or emotions through violent exertions of the will, even when momentarily successful, simply generates equally strong contrary reactions and is thus ultimately self-defeating. The pathological consequences – psychic and psychosomatic – of repressions and inhibitions have long been recognized in Western psychology and are only too familiar a part of our modern world. Effort *is*, of course, needed but should be focused exclusively on the development of stable, undistracted mindfulness. This is the task to which the maximum possible degree of energy must be devoted, so as to ensure an attitude of clear-sighted awareness, free from impulsive reactions. In this way the increasingly penetrating perception of the transitory and impersonal nature of all phenomena gradually weakens and dissolves the ingrained tendency to attachment (based on the delusion that there is a lasting 'self' whose wants have to be met) which is the root cause of the hindrances themselves. The experience of centuries has shown that progress in this connection takes place in several distinct stages, which will be discussed later (the four 'paths' and their respective 'fruits', in the traditional terminology[184]), and the various negative elements are eliminated one after another ('He knows how the non-arising in the future of the abandoned sense-desire, etc., comes to be').

2.5.1.2 *The Six Sense Bases (*salāyatana*) and the Fetters (*saṃyojana*) That Arise in Consequence*

And again, monks, a monk dwells contemplating mental objects in the mental objects [that are] the six internal and external sense-bases. And how does he contemplate? Here, monks, a monk knows the *eye*, knows *visible* objects and knows the fetter that arises dependent on both [the eye and visible objects] . . . , he knows the *ear* and *sounds* . . . , the *nose* and *smells* . . . , the *tongue* and *flavours* . . . , the *body* and *tactile objects* . . . , the *mind* and *mental objects*, and knows the fetter that arises dependent on both; he knows how the arising of the [previously] non-arisen fetter comes to be; he knows how the abandoning of the arisen fetter comes to be; and he knows how the non-arising in the future of the abandoned fetter comes to be.

This is a brief statement of how perception takes place. For perception to occur there has to be an organ (eye, ear, etc.), which is the 'internal sense-base', an object (visible form, sound, etc.), which is the 'external sense-base', and the contact or connection between the two (the eye looking at the physical object, the ear hearing a sound, etc.). But the Buddha's analysis, practical as always, does not stop at the mechanism of perception, but proceeds at once to consider its consequences, i.e. the 'fetters', which result from the act of perception because of our incorrect understanding, which interprets what is impermanent as lasting, what is empty as substantive, and what is impersonal as having a self.

In the Buddha's terminology, the 'fetters' are so called because they are the attitudes and states of mind which bind us to the unsatisfactory existence of an unenlightened person, dominated by attachment and by suffering. Here, too (as in the case of the hindrances), what is needed is to get to know these negative factors and to work towards their elimination ('He knows how the arising of the non-arisen fetter comes to be; he knows how the abandoning of the arisen fetter comes to be; and he knows how the non-arising in the future of the abandoned fetter comes to be'). The fetters are classified under ten headings:

1. Personality belief (i.e. the delusion that there is, in any real sense, such a thing as a 'self').

2. Doubt (about the correctness of the teaching, the effectiveness of the practice, etc.).

3. Attachment to rules and rituals (in the mistaken belief that rituals and external observances in themselves can help the progress of insight).

4. Craving for sensual satisfactions (i.e. for pleasant objects as perceived by the five bodily senses).

5. Ill will (i.e. aversion to whatever, at the physical or mental level, is perceived as disagreeable or threatening).

6. Craving for satisfactions at levels of pure form (traditionally also

called 'fine-material' states).

7. Craving for satisfactions at formless levels (traditionally, 'immaterial' states).

8. Conceit.

9. Restlessness.

10. Ignorance.

The sixth and seventh fetters arise in connection with the states of happiness, bliss and tranquillity which can be achieved with tranquillity meditation (*samatha*); the 'fine-material' states relate to the formal, and the 'immaterial' states to the formless absorptions.[185] The attachment to those states is more difficult to overcome than the attachment to ordinary material, sensual satisfactions, precisely because those states represent in themselves qualitatively very subtle and intensely satisfactory experiences. This is why, as will be seen later,[186] the definitive elimination of these two fetters (as well as of the three following ones) takes place only in the last stage of the progress of insight, when the meditator achieves the total realization of enlightenment.

2.5.1.3 *The Seven Factors of Enlightenment* (sambojjhanga)

And again, monks, a monk dwells contemplating mental objects in the mental objects [that are] the seven factors of enlightenment. And how does he contemplate? Here, monks, when the enlightenment factor of *mindfulness* is present in him, a monk knows: 'The enlightenment factor of mindfulness is in me'; or when the enlightenment factor of mindfulness is absent, he knows: 'The enlightenment factor of mindfulness is not in me.' And he knows how the arising of the [previously] non-arisen enlightenment factor of mindfulness comes to be; and he knows how perfection in the development of the arisen enlightenment factor of mindfulness comes to be.

When the enlightenment factor of *investigation of reality* . . . , *energy* . . . , *happiness* (or rapture) . . . , *tranquillity* . . . , *concentration* . . . , *equanimity* is present in him, a monk knows: 'The enlightenment factor of investigation of reality . . . , energy . . . , happiness . . . , tranquillity . . . , concentration . . . , equanimity is in me'; or when the enlightenment factor [of investigation of reality, etc.] is absent, he knows: 'The enlightenment factor [of investigation of reality, etc.] is not in me.' And he knows how the arising of the [previously] non-arisen enlightenment factor . . . comes to be; and he knows how perfection in the development of the arisen enlightenment factor . . . comes to be.

As in the previous exercise, there are two stages involved. First, the awareness of what is going on ('He knows: "The enlightenment factor of mindfulness, etc., is in me''; or when the enlightenment factor is absent, he knows: ''The enlightenment factor . . . is not in me'' '). Secondly, doing something about it: in the case of the hindrances, the task was to get rid of them; here, since the factors are positive, making for enlightenment, one has to try to preserve and develop them ('he knows how the arising of the non-arisen enlightenment factor . . . comes to be, and how perfection in the development of the arisen enlightenment factor . . . comes to be').

The order in which the factors of enlightenment are enumerated is not accidental, but reflects their mutual interrelationships. In fact, in the development of insight each one of them follows from the preceding factors and contributes to the establishment of the subsequent ones. This sequence is explained in very clear and simple terms in another of the Buddha's discourses:[187]

And how, monks, do the four foundations of mindfulness, developed and assiduously practised, perfect the seven factors of enlightenment?

Now when a monk dwells contemplating the body in the body . . . , sensations in the sensations . . . , the mind in the mind . . . , mental objects in mental objects, ardent, clearly comprehending and mindful, having overcome covetousness and grief concerning the world, then unremitting mindfulness is established in him. And when unremitting mindfulness is established in a monk, then the enlightenment factor of *mindfulness* is aroused in him, and he develops it, and through development it comes to perfection in him.

Dwelling thus mindful, he investigates and examines that state with understanding and embarks upon a scrutiny [of it]. When, dwelling thus mindful, a monk investigates and examines that state with understanding and embarks upon a scrutiny of it, then the enlightenment factor of *investigation of reality* is aroused in him, and he develops it, and through development it comes to perfection in him.

In him who investigates and examines that state with understanding and embarks upon a scrutiny of it, tireless energy is aroused. When tireless energy is aroused in a monk, who investigates and examines that state with understanding and embarks upon a scrutiny of it, then the enlightenment factor of *energy* is aroused in him, and he develops it, and through development it comes to perfection in him.

In him who has aroused energy, unworldly happiness[188] arises. When unworldly happiness arises in a monk who has aroused energy, then the enlightenment factor of *happiness* is aroused in him, and he develops it, and through development it comes to perfection in him.

The body and mind of one whose mind is happy become tranquil. When the body and mind of a monk whose mind is happy become tranquil, then the enlightenment factor of *tranquillity* is aroused in him, and he develops it, and through development it comes to perfection in him.

The mind of one who is tranquil in body and blissful becomes concentrated. When the mind of a monk who is tranquil in body and blissful becomes concentrated, then the enlightenment factor of *concentration* is aroused in him, and he develops it, and through development it comes to perfection in him. He becomes one who looks with complete equanimity on the mind thus concentrated. When a monk becomes one who looks with complete equanimity on the mind thus concentrated, then the enlightenment factor of *equanimity* is aroused in him, and he develops it, and through development it comes to perfection in him.

Thus developed, monks, thus assiduously practised, the four foundations of mindfulness perfect the seven factors of enlightenment.

In the same discourse, the Buddha stresses the capital importance of the factors of enlightenment, saying that 'the seven factors of enlightenment, developed and assiduously practised, produce the perfection of knowledge and deliverance'.

2.5.2 Analysis of Reality

2.5.2.1 The Five Aggregates of Clinging (upādāna-khandha)

And again, monks, a monk dwells contemplating mental objects in the mental objects [that are] the five aggregates of clinging. And how does he contemplate? Here, monks, a monk considers: 'Thus is material form, thus the arising of material form, thus the passing away of material form; thus is sensation, thus the arising of sensation, thus the passing away of sensation; thus is perception, thus the arising of perception, thus the passing away of perception; thus are mental formations, thus the arising of mental formations, thus the passing away of mental formations; thus is consciousness, thus the arising of consciousness, thus the passing away of consciousness.'

These five 'aggregates' or groups of phenomena (i.e. matter, sensation, perception, mental formations or activity and consciousness) comprehend, in the Buddha's teaching, everything that makes up the cognizable universe.

All material phenomena, whether past, present or future, one's own or external, gross or subtle, lofty or low, far or near, all belong to the aggregate of material form. All sensations . . . belong to the aggregate of sensation. All perceptions . . . belong to the aggregate of perception. All mental formations . . . belong to the aggregate of mental formations. All consciousness . . . belongs to the aggregate of consciousness.[189]

The five aggregates of clinging include therefore also, by definition, all those physical and mental phenomena which to the untrained person appear to constitute his or her 'self' or 'personality' and to which one clings in an effort to preserve the essentially illusory configuration which one calls 'myself'. This is why they are called aggregates of *clinging*.

Now, as we have seen, the purpose of *vipassanā* meditation is precisely to develop insight into the actual nature of these phenomena, and so to see and understand that they are all transient, unstable events, without lasting identity. In this exercise the meditator maintains a mental attitude of mindful receptiveness, a truly 'open mind', and contemplates whatever arises in the field of perception from moment to moment, endeavouring to be clearly aware of the category or 'aggregate' to which each phenomenon belongs. When he becomes aware of a material phenomenon, he simply makes a mental note of 'materiality' or 'material form'; when a sensation arises, he notes whether it is 'pleasant, unpleasant or neutral'; when a perception occurs (i.e. when there is an awareness of the kind of phenomenon[190]), he notes both its general characteristic (i.e. whether it is visual, auditory, olfactory, gustatory, tactile or mental) and its specificity (e.g. a flower, a shout, a kitchen smell); when contemplating mental activity, he notes its source or origin and its character (mental reactions or associations of ideas arising in connection with different material or mental objects); and when contemplating consciousness itself, he notes the particular state of consciousness obtaining at that moment (that is to say, the type of exercise that was described under the contemplation of the mind or mental states under section 2.4 above).

What is absolutely essential, as in all *vipassanā* exercises, is to proceed without attachment, dispassionately, without either desiring or rejecting, remaining always aware of the fact that what is being inspected are configurations of changing phenomena, always arising and passing away ('he considers: "Thus is material form, etc., . . . thus the arising . . . , thus the passing away of material form, etc." '). In this way, the meditator is putting into practice the exact injunctions of the oft-repeated 'Compendium of Practice':

He dwells contemplating the arising of phenomena . . . , or the passing away of phenomena . . . , or the arising and passing away of phenomena in mental objects. Or the mindfulness that 'there are mental objects' is established in him to the extent necessary for knowledge and mindfulness. . . . Thus, indeed, monks, a monk dwells contemplating mental objects in the mental objects [that are] the five aggregates of clinging.

This exercise, combining the practice of non-reactive awareness with the dispassionate discrimination of phenomena, is particularly helpful in developing a thorough understanding of the fundamental truth that material form is transient, sensation is transient, perception is transient, mental formations are transient, consciousness is transient. And that which is transient is subject to suffering [as long as we persist in clinging to things and wanting to hold up their ceaseless flow], and of that which is transient and subject to suffering and change, one cannot rightly say: 'This belongs to me, this am I, this is my self.'[191]

2.5.2.2 *The Four Noble Truths* (ariya sacca)

And again, monks, a monk dwells contemplating mental objects in the mental objects [that are] the four noble truths. And how does he contemplate? Here, monks, a monk knows according to reality: 'This is suffering'; he knows according to reality: 'This is the origin of suffering'; he knows according to reality: 'This is the cessation of suffering'; he knows according to reality: 'This is the way leading to the cessation of suffering.'

These are the Four Noble Truths which sum up the essence of the Buddha's teaching, and it will be recalled that they were briefly discussed in chapter 2. The present exercise consists in taking as subjects for contemplation the Four Truths as constantly manifested in the workings and contents of our minds. This is a contemplation which can be carried out at different levels (depending on the meditator's mentality and degree of proficiency), producing extraordinarily deep and subtle insights, but I can do no more at this point than briefly illustrate it by means of a very simple example.

Whatever unpleasant mental phenomenon arises in the course of meditation (either in connection with physical pain or discomfort, or as a mental occurrence on its own) is, obviously, *suffering* (the first truth) and needs to be immediately identified as such. The skilled meditator, however, knows that the phenomenon as such, the sensory-mental input, has no intrinsic quality – it is the perceiving and evaluating part of the mind that labels it as 'unpleasant', by *reacting* in a specific manner (rejection) to a phenomenon which is perceived as, in some way, a threat or an aggression. This rejection, this 'not wanting' (suffering, discomfort, etc.), is *the origin of suffering* (the second truth). Now when the meditator becomes aware of this reaction (provided that the awareness is really strong and clear), he thereby ceases to identify with it. His experience is no longer one of unreflecting reaction, but rather one of dispassionate observation of the emergent reaction; he no longer 'wants' (to stop the pain, discomfort or whatever), but simply observes and notes. To stop 'wanting' is to stop reacting – and this is *the cessation of suffering* (the third truth). A banal example of this (but one which is particularly striking precisely because it is so obvious and so easily experienced by anyone who tries) is the matter of the aches and pains in the joints and muscles which almost invariably assail novice meditators when they have to sit perfectly motionless for unaccustomedly long periods of formal sitting meditation. With a little practice it is everyone's experience that, when contemplated with scrupulous mindfulness and without emotion, they cease to be perceived as 'pains' and one discovers in them a whole range of varied physical sensations (prickling, pressure, tension, etc.) which *in themselves* have nothing to do with the concept of 'pain' and which, like all sensations, are in a state of flux – changing, disappearing and being replaced by others. Finally the meditator comes to realize that, by practising correctly with care and dedication, he is putting into practice one or more of the eight component factors of *the way leading to the cessation of suffering* (the fourth truth), not only during meditation periods (when, with right view and right purpose, he applies right effort to develop right mindfulness and right concentration), but also in the intervals between sessions during a course or retreat (right view, right purpose, right effort, right speech, right action, right mindfulness), and also – in between courses or retreats – in his daily life, to the extent that he is increasingly inspired and guided by the healthy principles that he has learned and practised (guided by a right view of things, pursuing a right purpose, practising right speech and right action on every occasion, earning a living in the right kind of occupation, and exerting right effort to maintain and develop this kind of life).

2.6 *Conclusion of the Discourse on the Foundations of Mindfulness*

In truth, monks, whoever practises these four Foundations of Mindfulness in this manner for seven years may expect one of two fruits: highest knowledge [arahantship] here and now or, if some remainder of clinging is still present, the state of 'non-return'.

Let alone seven years, monks! Should a person practise these four Foundations of Mindfulness in this manner for six years . . . , five . . . , four . . . , three . . . , two years . . . , for one year, he may expect one of two fruits: highest knowledge here and now or, if some remainder of clinging is still present, the state of 'non-return'.

Let alone one year, monks! Should a person practise these four Foundations of Mindfulness in this manner for seven months . . . , six . . . , five . . . , four . . . , three . . . , two months . . . , one month . . . , half a month . . . , seven days, he may expect one of two fruits: highest knowledge here and now or, if some remainder of clinging is still present, the state of 'non-return'.

This is why it has been said: 'This is the only way, monks, for the purification of beings, for the overcoming of sorrow and lamentation, for the destroying of pain and grief, for reaching the right path, for the realization of *nibbāna*, namely the four Foundations of Mindfulness.' Thus spoke the Blessed One. Glad at heart, the monks rejoiced at his words.

The discourse thus ends as it began – with a solemn statement of the capital importance of the practices it teaches to achieve the full realization of nirvana (*nibbāna*). Before saying what little can be said about this ultimate achievement, which, as I have said before, is something that can be experienced but not talked about, it is necessary to look a little more closely at the above quotation. Everything that is said there, as elsewhere in the discourse (and in the Buddha's teaching generally) is not at all a piece of generally inspirational rhetoric but conveys a very specific practical meaning to the properly informed reader. Thus, the apparently rhetorical reference to years, months, etc., of practice makes the very true and important point that the rate of progress that can be expected varies considerably from person to person. What one may achieve in a matter of days may take another months or years. It all depends on each individual's mentality, character and abilities, as well as his particular life situation. In traditional Buddhist terms, in other words, it depends on the present load of karmic results – beneficial or harmful, favourable or unfavourable – accumulated from previous mental, verbal or physical actions. Secondly, it stresses the fact that realization is achieved not all at once but (as was pointed out before[192]) in successive stages. This is what the passage is about which refers to two results, or fruits, that may be expected of practice as 'highest knowledge here and now or, if some remainder of clinging is still present, the state of "non-return" '. This brief allusion was, of course, quite sufficient for the monks who were the original hearers of the discourse and were wholly conversant with the relevant frame of reference. For the modern, non-specialized reader, however, some explanation is required.

2.6.1 *The Process of Purification*

In the Buddha's teaching the process which, in today's language, we tend to describe in terms of 'realization' or 'integration' is traditionally known as *purification* (hence the title of the ancient meditation manual to which I have so often turned: *Visuddhi Magga* means 'Path of Purification'). This is a very appropriate term, since it stresses the fact that, in order to achieve the enduring transmutation of the human psyche that we have been talking about, what is needed can best be described as a cleansing process. Our mental and affective processes have to be gradually freed from the deeply ingrained habits of perception and reaction which prevent us from seeing and experiencing things as they really are (as illustrated, for instance, in the simile of the pond). In describing the contemplation of mental objects, we saw the main negative factors which each one of us has to eliminate through his own efforts: the mental hindrances and fetters. And it is precisely the mental fetters which – according to the traditional method – provide the necessary benchmarks, depending on the extent to which they have been weakened or eliminated, against which to measure progress along the path of purification.

2.6.1.1 Stream Entry

The first significant stage is signalled by the elimination of the first three fetters: *personality belief* (i.e. attachment to an illusory self), *doubt* (abou the efficacy of the teaching and practice) and the *attachment to rules and rituals* (which is a way, very commonly resorted to, of shirking the hard task of working on oneself). Someone who, through the development of insight, has done away with these three fetters, is called *sotāpanna* – literally, 'stream-enterer' – because he has achieved the first stage of a process which, flowing now irreversibly like a stream, will lead on to definitive enlightenment, i.e. *nibbāna*, after no more than seven rebirths at the most.

At this point, and in order to prevent any confusion, let us stop for a moment and consider the precise meaning of 'rebirth' and of the round of rebirths in Buddhism.

2.6.1.2 The Round of Rebirths

When speaking of rebirth people tend commonly to think in terms of a soul passing on, as a complete entity, into a new body at the death of its old one. This is what is known as reincarnation, transmigration or metempsychosis, and is a common belief in many Eastern religions (especially within the orthodox Hindu tradition) as well as in esoteric traditions in the West. In view of the fact that, as the Buddha taught, there is no such thing as a permanent self-entity to be found anywhere (see also chapter 2 above), it will be readily appreciated that it is a gross error to assimilate the Buddhist conception of 'rebirth' to that of 'transmigration of souls' (an error which is, regrettably, quite often fallen into even by supposedly well-informed authors, who fail to make this crucial distinction either through actual ignorance or through a partisan tendency to assimilate Buddhism to orthodox mainstream Hinduism).

In fact, the concept of transmigration or reincarnation necessarily presupposes the existence of a soul as a lasting entity which moves on from one mortal body to another without losing its own essence or entity. But, as has been seen, *this lasting entity is precisely what the Buddha found to be ultimately nonexistent*, an insight formulated in the fundamental principle of *anattā*. This principle, namely that there is no such thing anywhere as a permanent self-entity, is valid not only at the physical level (where transience and decay are only too evident) but equally so at all other levels, however they may be described – physical, mental, spiritual. The Buddha taught, and this is the very core of his teaching, that absolutely everything (*including* the unconditioned *nibbāna*) is without abiding entity or substance, without self, *anattā*. Hence the use of the word 'rebirth' which, by not prejudging the issue of *what* it is exactly that is reborn, is less loaded with the erroneous 'soul' connotation than those other terms.

On the other hand, however, the Buddha denied with equal energy the purely materialistic view, i.e. that the death of the body, the dissolution of the physical elements, represents the final annihilation of all the mental, volitional and affective elements which were also part of the organism that has died. This is why he taught that the first fetter, i.e. *personality belief*, arises in two equally mistaken and noxious forms, *eternalism* (the idealist delusion that there is such a thing as an abiding self or an immortal soul) and *annihilationism* (the materialist delusion that the end of a particular body is the end of everything). According to the Buddha, what happens is that the configuration of the psyche at the moment of death (itself the conditioned product of physical and mental acts performed in the existence which is now ending, as well as in previous ones) constitutes the initial consciousness, the starting point, as it were, of the next existence.

In other words, one could say, very roughly, that what is 'reborn' in the next life is the sediment, the psychical residue (of mental, volitional and affective material) of the current life and of previous ones in so far as their residues have not yet been worked through. The consciousness of the new being is therefore not the same as that of the previous one; it is not identical with it, but neither is it independent from it since it is, in fact, its consequence.

There is, therefore, no question of a soul which changes bodies as a body changes clothes. There is no transmigration of a permanent entity. This is why terms like 'reincarnation' must be eschewed, and it is preferable to use the more neutral term 'rebirth' which, without necessarily implying a permanent entity, signals that there is a continuity in diversity. The classic illustration of this process in the old Buddhist texts is the simile of a tree and its fruit: the seed contained in the fruit gives rise to another tree of the same kind as the original one. The new tree, obviously, is very similar to its parent, having inherited a particular set of genetic characteristics. These, however, unfold and develop in different ways, depending on circumstances such as the quality of the soil, the kind of climate and environmental conditions in general. The new tree thus carries on the characteristics of the previous one but in its own distinctive manner. It is always *another* tree. It is a descendant of the parent tree but not its 'reincarnation'. This is why in the Buddhist tradition it is said that beings are 'heirs to their *kamma* (actions of the body, speech and mind)'. Bearing this well in mind, let us now return to the process of purification.

2.6.1.3 *Once-Return*

The fourth and fifth fetters, i.e. the *craving for sensual satisfactions* and *physical or mental aversion*, demand a great deal of work to be fully eliminated. This is natural enough, since they are the very stuff of our untutored everyday existence.

Thus, the second stage of progress consists in substantially loosening the hold of these two fetters, but without yet achieving their entire removal. The person who, by assiduous practice of the eightfold path in all its aspects – ethical discipline, practice of meditation and development of understanding – has reduced to a minimum the influence of desire and aversion on his motivations, thoughts and actions, is called *sakādāgami*, which means 'once-returner'. He will be reborn only one more time in the world of mind and matter of human existence and will achieve definitive liberation in that last life.

2.6.1.4 *Non-Return*

When *sense desire* and all kinds of *aversion* or *ill will* have been entirely eliminated, the resulting state is known as that of *anāgāmi*, or 'non-returner'. This means that, being now entirely free from the first five fetters, consciousness is free from all attachment to the material world. If physical death occurs before the person has achieved the next and final stage, that is to say definitive enlightenment or *nibbāna*, this consciousness, having attained a high degree of freedom, is no longer reborn in a physical environment. Since it is, however, still conditioned by the karmic effects resulting from the five remaining fetters, it is reborn within a certain class of higher states of existence, from where it achieves *nibbāna* directly when the five remaining fetters have been eliminated.

The full range of higher states comprises the various levels of existence of discarnate intelligences which are recognized in all religious traditions, although under different names: angels, spirits, genii, devas, etc. As has been explained in chapter 4 (section 4.3.6), however, the essential difference between the Buddha's teaching and all other doctrines is that in the former it is never claimed that such states – no matter how sublime, lasting and beatific they may be as compared to the ordinary human condition – are to be considered as definitive or eternal. As the Buddha realized and taught, absolutely every conceivable thing, state or condition, with the only exception of *nibbāna* (which is undescribable and inconceivable), is transient. All paradises come to an end. Even 'angels' have to move on from their exalted sphere once the karmic consequences which brought them there are exhausted. If they were *anāgāmis*, then, without any further rebirth anywhere, they achieve *nibbāna*.

2.6.1.5 *Arahantship*

The last stage in the process is that in which the subtler and more insidious fetters are extirpated: the *craving for experiential levels of pure form* and of *formlessness* (which may occur as attachment and clinging to the extremely subtle and deep satisfactions of the altered states of consciousness of the formal and formless levels of *samatha* meditation, or as desires for rebirth in a 'paradise', i.e. in one of those immaterial states as variously conceived in religious cosmologies); *conceit* (which, in both senses of the word, is so deeply rooted in human nature, as the vanity of self and as the conceptualizing habit of the human mind); *restlessness* (existential anguish); and *ignorance* (which, by definition, persists to some extent as long as full insight has not been achieved).

The person who achieves this definitive liberation is called *arahant*, a term sometimes translated as 'holy one' but which literally means 'worthy' or 'deserving'. The *arahant*, indeed, is deserving of the utmost praise and recognition (not least as an inspirational model to be emulated) as having achieved the ultimate degree of freedom and perfection that is *nibbāna*. During the remainder of his lifetime the *arahant* enjoys what is known as '*nibbāna* with elements of existence' (*saupādisesa nibbāna*) and at death there is the achievement of *parinibbāna* or '*nibbāna* without elements of existence' (*anupādisesa nibbāna*), and what was known as the *arahant* disappears from the round of rebirths, in the old phrase, 'like a flame that has exhausted its fuel'.

2.6.1.6 *Summing Up*

Now we can go back to the discourse and understand the full import of the phrase which says that from the practice of the four foundations of mindfulness one may expect one of two results: 'highest knowledge here and now' – that is to say, arahantship – 'or, if some remainder of clinging is still present [i.e. if the last five fetters have not yet been eliminated], the state of "non-return".'

Notice that the Buddha refers here only to the last two of the four stages that make up the process of purification. This may partly be due to the fact that the discourse was originally addressed to experienced monks, direct disciples of the Buddha himself, most of whom had probably already attained the first two stages.

There is, however, another reason which I believe to be more fundamental. By placing as an aim before the student, directly, 'the highest knowledge' of definitive attainment or, as the alternative, the already very advanced stage that comes immediately before it, the discourse stresses something which the Buddha repeated on many occasions, namely that the attainment of *nibbāna* is not something that lies in some distant, hopeful future after who knows how many rebirths, but something which can be achieved – if one is prepared to work hard at it – 'here and now' in this very existence. Of course, it is an arduous endeavour and may indeed require, depending on each person's burden of negative accumulations, more than one or two lives. But this should be no excuse for not putting maximum enthusiasm and perseverance into doing as much as one can in this present life which is, after all, the only thing we have to work on for the time being. *Nibbāna* is for today – not for tomorrow. The present moment must be taken advantage of calmly, without self-defeating anxiety or haste, but also without weakening. And, the Buddha says in effect, if we proceed as instructed in this discourse, practising the foundations of mindfulness assiduously, we shall attain the goal, or very nearly. Another point which should be taken into account in this connection is that the four stages or levels which have just been described do not follow one upon the other in a rigid time sequence. That is to say, depending on the capacities, disposition, energy and enthusiasm of each practitioner, moving on from one to the next level may take a whole life, years or months, or may be just a matter of minutes. It is a well-known fact that mental processes can unfold at tremendous speeds, and it is thus not surprising to find numerous examples in the old texts of persons who being, for instance, already stream-enterers (*sotāpanna*), became *arahants* almost instantly, under particularly favourable circumstances, telescoping the intervening stages. As in so many things, it is the first step that is most difficult, i.e. managing to extricate oneself from the state of uncontrolled impulses and perceptual confusion which characterizes the initial mentality of most of us, and 'entering the stream'. Even there, however, examples of rapid progress are far from infrequent.

One more explanation seems in order, concerning the fact that (as mentioned at the end of section 2.5.1.1 of this chapter) traditional Buddhist terminology distinguishes, in connection with the four stages of progress, the four 'paths' (*magga*) and their respective 'fruits' (*phala*). These are terms that recur very frequently in Buddhist texts and it is important that they should be clearly understood. To go into this matter in detail would require a discussion of the *Abhidhamma* (the section of the original Pali canon which elaborates the philosophical and, most particularly, psychological aspects of the Buddha's teaching). Quite simply, however, it may be said that the 'paths' and their 'fruits' refer to the way in which the emergence of higher states of consciousness takes place in the progress of insight. In each of the four stages described the attainment of the characteristic state of consciousness is instantaneous – there is a moment of *access*, and this moment is called the 'path'. Immediately thereafter there follows the *experience* of the new state, and this is the 'fruit'. An extract from the relevant entry in the *Buddhist Dictionary*, the Venerable Nyānatiloka's fundamental work of reference,[193] will help to make this clear:

According to the *Abhidhamma*, 'supermundane path' or simply 'Path' (*magga*) is a designation of the moment of entering into one of the 4 stages of holiness [that is to say, the four stages I have just enumerated, starting with stream-entry] – Nirvana being the object – produced by intuitional Insight (*vipassanā*) into the impermanency, misery and impersonality of existence, flashing forth and for ever transforming one's life and nature. By 'Fruition' (*phala*) are meant those moments of consciousness which follow immediately thereafter as the result of the Path, and which in certain circumstances may repeat for innumerable times during life-time.

(I) Through the Path of Stream-Winning (*sotāpatti-magga*) one 'becomes' free (whereas in realizing the fruition, one 'is' free) from the first 3 fetters (*saṃyojana, q.v.*) which bind beings to existence in the sensuous sphere . . . [and similarly for the other stages].

One last word of warning. It has sometimes been thought that to practise correctly one should undertake, one after the other, *all* the exercises mentioned in the discourse, beginning with mindfulness of breath and ending with the mental objects. This is not the case. Some of the exercises are more generally suitable for all types of persons (such as mindfulness of breathing, which is the most universal of all), while others should rather be reserved for certain types of mentality. But – provided one practises properly, i.e. that one is 'ardent, clearly comprehending and mindful, having overcome covetousness and grief concerning the world', as the discourse insists time and again – each exercise is quite enough in itself to achieve the goal. It is in order to make this quite clear that the 'Compendium of Practice' repeated in each individual section of the discourse specifies that the meditator 'dwells contemplating the arising of phenomena . . . , the passing away of phenomena . . . , and the arising and passing away of phenomena. . . . Or the mindfulness that "there is/are body . . . , sensations . . . , mind . . . , mental objects" is established in him *to the extent necessary for knowledge and mindfulness.*' The whole point being precisely to *experience* with fully mindful awareness the arising and passing away of all phenomena, to live the experience of total impermanence, so as to achieve in this way the non-mediated, experiential knowledge which is freedom.

This on the one hand. On the other, however, it must be clearly understood that, while each exercise is enough in itself for use as the main or basic exercise in formal training, its practice also involves that of the others to some extent. This is so because, as has already been explained, certain exercises are sometimes deliberately used as complements, in conjunction with the main one, during a course of training (as, for instance, formal walking meditation alternating with periods of sitting meditation), and also because one endeavours to maintain the highest possible level of mindful awareness while performing ordinary tasks in between meditation periods (by maintaining clear comprehension of all one's actions, thoughts, etc.).

But there is a more fundamental reason. Quite simply, since all life processes – mental as well as physical – are intimately connected with one another, there cannot fail to be a natural, continual interplay between the four foundations of mindfulness (body, sensations, mind and mental contents), a mutual feedback which fluctuates with the flow of phenomena, but is always present to a greater or lesser extent.

The most obvious connection is the close relationship between the contemplation of the body and that of sensations (to which reference was already made in section 2.3 of this chapter). But mental states and mental contents, too, have their physical correlates and, conversely, bodily processes and events have an effect on the mind and the emotions (one trembles with fear, taking a few deep breaths helps to calm jittery nerves, etc.). The practice of mindful observation must take all this into account, since the whole point of the exercise (whatever foundation of mindfulness it may be practised on) is precisely to maintain full awareness of whatever is present 'here and now' and to observe it dispassionately. When discussing the contemplation of the mind (in section 2.4 of this chapter), it was pointed out that the awareness of mental states must also be maintained during the contemplation of the body in order to ensure unbroken mindfulness. If a sudden feeling of anxiety or of elation arises and is not consciously noted at once, the meditator is not paying proper attention.

This is why in another very famous discourse, the *Ānāpānasatisutta*, or *Discourse on Mindfulness of Breathing*,[194] the Buddha devoted a whole course of instruction to explaining how the exclusive practice of mindfulness of breathing, used as the main exercise, perfects the other foundations of mindfulness and thus leads (in a certain sense by itself but, in fact, involving the whole spectrum of possible objects) to the ultimate achievement.

Very briefly, the discourse explains that mindfulness of breathing is, as we know, contemplation of the body; that paying close attention to the quality of the sensations which arise during breathing is contemplation of the sensations; that paying attention to accompanying mental states is contemplation of the mind; and that paying attention to mental contents and, in particular, to the appreciation of the impermanence, of the arising and passing away of phenomena as perceived with mindful awareness, is contemplation of mental objects. Thus, says the Buddha,

mindfulness of breathing, developed and assiduously practised, perfects the four foundations of mindfulness; the four foundations of mindfulness, developed and assiduously practised, perfect the seven factors of enlightenment; and the seven factors of enlightenment, developed and assiduously practised, produce the perfection of knowledge and deliverance.

7
The Ultimate: Nibbāna

After considering at some length the ways and means of achieving that supremely desirable end that is *nibbāna*,[195] one might well expect some more explicit information about the goal itself. The problem here is that, as has already been pointed out more than once, the very nature of *nibbāna* is such as to preclude an analytic or descriptive explanation. The ultimate achievement taught by the Buddha is inexplicable, in the literal sense of the word, because it does not fall within the verbal-conceptual categories that we are bound to use for intellectual communication and understanding. Consequently, every effort to explain *nibbāna* within the framework of these categories, every attempt to apprehend it conceptually, is, by definition, pointless. It is also inevitably misleading since, in trying to fit the inexplicable into some kind of intellectually understandable mould – i.e. into some kind of, literally, 'conceivable' category – all that happens (and it has happened time and again in the history of Buddhist thought) is that it is 'explained' by being subjected to all sorts of philosophical, religious and linguistic deformations, all of them conditioned by the cultural environment or tradition from which they spring.

Thus one finds, at the more superficial level, the facile identifications of 'nirvana' as simply a paradise (essentially similar to those of Christian or Moslem eschatology), as a mystic union with the godhead, as the realization of the Ātman/Brahman identity (as in Vedānta Hinduism), or as a total annihilation. A variety of more or less sophisticated 'interpretations' along such lines has been propounded not only by Western students of Buddhism but also, down the centuries, by Buddhists themselves of the kind who were more inclined to speculate than to practise *vipassanā.* So, *nibbāna* 'with elements of existence' *(saupādisesa nibbāna)* has been variously interpreted as a metaphysical experience, as a mystic experience, as a hypnotic state, as a temporary annihilation, as a state of superconsciousness (of an absolute All, or of an absolute Nothing); and *nibbāna* 'without elements of existence' *(anupādisesa nibbāna),* i.e. upon the dissolution of the body, as a state of conscious bliss, as a paradisical eternity, as eternal sleep, as annihilation pure and simple, as a merging back into an absolute Ground, as a definitive union with a Supreme Consciousness, as the annihilation of the 'self' in the realization of the 'Self', etc.[196]

All this is in striking contrast to the Buddha's own attitude; he abstained from theorizing and metaphysical speculation, and considered the great themes which have traditionally exercised the minds of philosophers and religious thinkers as unprofitable questions best left unanswered, on which people waste precious time which they could devote, with much greater profit, to the practice of *vipassanā* (remember the simile of the poisoned arrow quoted at the beginning of chapter 2). The questions as to whether the world is eternal or not eternal, finite or infinite, as to whether there is soul, or a life principle which is identical or not identical with the body, of whether he who has achieved *nibbāna* goes on existing in some way after the death of the body, or does not go on existing – all such questions, said the Buddha, are nothing but a pursuit of and a clinging to mere views, 'a thicket of views, a puppet-show of views, a toil of views, a snare of views'.[197] They do not help us in any way to achieve that 'unshakeable deliverance of the mind' which, he never tired of repeating, 'is the object of the holy life, its essence, its goal'.[198]

However, since words have to be used for purposes of communication, even the Buddha himself sometimes could not avoid having to say *something* about *nibbāna* (usually in order to refute mistaken views about it). When compelled to do so, the Buddha would resort only to the simplest, soberest terms: *nibbāna,* and this is the crux of the matter, is *the end of suffering.* No other positive statement can usefully be made about it.

On the other hand, one can go on at some length about what *nibbāna* is *not,* in order to try and discourage the proliferation of 'interpretations' – which are all, in one way or another, reductionist – and clearly to establish its unique character and the one fact that it has nothing to do with all that makes up the conceivable universe:

There is, monks, something which is neither earth, nor water, nor fire, nor air, neither boundless space nor boundless consciousness, nor nothingness, nor the state of neither-perception-nor-non-perception; neither this world nor another world, neither sun nor moon. That, monks, I call neither coming nor going, nor remaining, neither dying nor being born. It is without support, development or foundation. That is the end of suffering.[199]

As we have had occasion to note before, the Buddha did not go in for rhetoric but was always intent on conveying quite specific, concrete information. This passage, too, far from being (as it has too often been taken to be) one of those solemn utterances which aim to awe and impress rather than to foster understanding, does in fact convey some carefully specific meanings. Let us take a close look at it.

It begins, obviously enough, by dissociating *nibbāna* from the realm of physical matter, by stating that it has no connection with any of the four primordial elements (earth, water, fire and air) of which, according to ancient tradition, matter is composed. Then the realm of metaphysics, of that which is beyond physical matter, is equally excluded: we are told that neither boundless space nor boundless consciousness can be predicated of *nibbāna*; nor can one say that it is nothingness; nor even that it is a state where there is neither perception nor non-perception. The denial of any connection between *nibbāna* and anything that can be conceived is, as can be seen, rising to ever more rarefied levels. In addition, however, it should be clearly noted that these last four categories also have a perfectly concrete psychological (not metaphysical) meaning in the Buddha's teaching. They refer to the levels of experience attained in the four formless absorptions of *samatha* meditation.[200] By pointing out that they are not related to *nibbāna*, the Buddha here stresses that it is not the practice of tranquillity meditation that leads to ultimate insight and enlightenment.

There follows then a series of further negatives, which are all meant to stress, quite uncompromisingly, that *nibbāna* belongs to a different dimension from that in which our intellectual apprehension of things – which proceeds always by opposites – operates: we think in terms of yes/no, life/death, here/there, time/eternity, etc. But *nibbāna* has nothing to do either with 'this world nor another world', has nothing to do with 'coming or going or remaining' (note here the dovetailing of two sets of oppositions: coming/going, and coming-or-going/remaining), nothing to do with 'dying or being born'. In other words, the mechanism of opposites, of either/or, does not apply to it. Therefore, it cannot be stated that because 'it is without support, development or foundation' it is simply 'nothing', since the concept of 'nothing' is also part of the either/or dimension (something/nothing). In any event, the relevance of the concept of 'nothingness' to *nibbāna* has already been denied earlier on in the quotation. The assimilation of *nibbāna* to 'nothing', i.e. the annihilationist view of the Buddha's teaching, has, however, always been a tempting one for those who approach the teaching from the outside (i.e. attempting an intellectual understanding, but without practising it). It was, in fact, one of the objections most commonly levelled against the Buddha's teaching by other religious leaders of his time. It was to show that the objection was unfounded that, on another occasion, the Buddha emphatically declared:

There is, monks, something that is not born, not originated, not made, not compound. For, monks, were there not this which is not born, not originated, not made, not compound, then no escape would be known from what is born, originated, made, compound. But, monks, since there is something that is not born, not originated, not made, not compound, therefore an escape is known from what is born, originated, made, compound.[201]

The sense of these words must be carefully investigated. Here the Buddha states categorically that 'there is something that is not born, etc.' and that therefore there is 'an escape from what is born, etc.', i.e. that there is such a thing as *nibbāna* which, as we know, is the end of the suffering inherent in all that is born, etc. *Nibbāna* is not simply 'nothing' (a category which, as we have just seen, is in any case not applicable to this issue), and the Buddha explains once again that it is 'something' different from the world of mind and matter with which we are familiar. This time he formulates the distinction in the broadest and most comprehensive terms possible. Earlier on he made it clear that *nibbāna* was neither physical nor metaphysical. Now he tells us that it has nothing to do with any aspect whatsoever of the web of interrelations, of causes and effects, mental and material, which constitutes our perceived universe. Everything that exists – from galaxies to viruses, from mathematical concepts to the most primitive instinctual drives – is, in one way or another, born, originated or made, and certainly compound (i.e. made up of a variety of component parts of processes). In this sense, *nibbāna* does not exist. But it is nevertheless something real and accessible to experiential knowledge ('were there not this which is not born . . . then an escape from what is born . . . would not be known here. But since there is something that is not born . . . therefore an escape from what is born . . . is known').

Nevertheless, as just pointed out, both in the Buddha's own time and on many occasions since then, such a categorical affirmation has not deterred people who were unable or unwilling to accept the reality of 'something' as conceptually undefinable as this *nibbāna* from labelling the Buddha's teaching as nihilism pure and simple. They have sought support for this view in the etymology of the term itself, since both the Sanskrit *nirvāna* and the Pali *nibbāna* are derived from the combination of the negative prefix *nir* with the root *vā* (to blow), so that *nirvāna* or *nibbāna* is 'to cease blowing' or to become extinguished, like a flame that lacks oxygen.[202] The Buddha's answer to this was:

In one sense it may be rightly said of me: 'The monk Gotama is a nihilist, he teaches the doctrine of annihilation and trains his disciples therein.' I teach the annihilation of greed, hate and delusion, I teach the annilihation of the many evil and unwholesome things. In this sense it may be rightly said of me that: 'The monk Gotama is a nihilist, and teaches the doctrine of annihilation, and instructs his disciples therein.'[203]

And he solemnly affirmed the positive value of *nibbāna* in terms of peace and supreme achievement:

This is peace, this is the highest, namely the end of all formations, the forsaking of every substratum of existence, the extinction of craving, fading away, cessation, *nibbāna*.[204]

Let us consider this statement which, once again, is not poetically inspirational but concretely informative. 'All formations' (*sankhāra*) refers to all that is compound and conditioned, that is to say, everything that is subsumed in the five aggregates of clinging which (as explained in section 2.5.2.1 of chapter 6) comprise all that can be perceived and cognized, all of which is impermanent and, in consequence, a source of suffering so long as we persist in clinging to it. These aggregates, together with the whole network of causes and effects to which they give rise, constitute the 'substrata of existence' which, in the Buddha's teaching, are considered to be four:

1. The *five aggregates of clinging* themselves.

2. *Sense desire*, involving the whole game of 'wanting' and 'not wanting' which is the root cause of suffering.

3. The so-called *ten defilements* (which, like all these classifications, is another way of bringing together – for purposes of explanation and teaching – the main obstacles and unwholesome qualities that we have to overcome in ourselves; it will be noted that some of them have already appeared under other groupings). These are: *greed*, *hate* and *delusion* (the three 'roots of existence', greed and hate being the two aspects of attachment – wanting/not wanting – which itself springs from delusion, from the misunderstanding

of what is impermanent as lasting, and consequent craving for it), *conceit* (seen before as one of the fetters) and *speculative views* (which arise in consequence of the fetter of ignorance), *doubt* (also classified elsewhere as a fetter and as a hindrance), *sloth* and *agitation* (another two of the five hindrances) and, finally, two ethical aspects, *shamelessness* (described as 'lack of moral shame', unscrupulousness), and *lack of moral fear* (i.e. not fearing the nefarious consequences, for oneself and for others, of evil, harmful behaviour).

4. *Kamma*: it is important to understand that *kamma* (or *karma*, which is the Sanskrit form of the word that has become accepted in Western languages) means *act*. Specifically, *kamma* is a volition, an act of the will, with its attendant mental and affective factors. The act may not go beyond the mental sphere (wish, intention, disposition, etc.), or it may become manifest in words and deeds, but at all these levels (even at the purely mental, unmanifested one) it is always an act, always *kamma*, involving – through the law of cause and effect – certain consequences (*kamma vipāka*, literally, 'ripening of the act') which condition our subsequent existence.

Then the Buddha stresses the essential point: what needs to be achieved is 'the extinction of craving' – this craving which, with its attendant attachment, is the root and source of our problems (remember what was said on the subject in chapter 2, section 3.2) – 'fading away and cessation'. 'Fading away' is the more literal translation of the important term *virāga* (quite literally, 'losing colour') and points both to the fact that all phenomena fade away or pass away, and also to the fading away of one's desire for, and attachment to, these transient phenomena as one gradually realizes, through direct experiential understanding, their impermanent nature. It is because of this latter sense that the Pali term is often also translated as 'detachment' or 'dispassion'. But, as this tends to leave aside one of the two connotations, it seems preferable to be more literal, even though 'fading away' may sound somewhat strange at first.

As for 'cessation' (*nirodha*), a frequent synonym of *nibbāna*, this is, of course, the cessation of delusion and of ignorance through the full understanding of the ephemeral nature of 'all formations'. As soon as this is really and truly understood, attachment ceases entirely, since it is seen that there is, quite literally, nothing to be attached to. With the cessation of attachment there is no further anxiety, anguish and unhappiness. This is the end of suffering. This is *nibbāna*.

The fact that no satisfactory conceptual formulation can be offered concerning the essence or intrinsic nature of *nibbāna* does not mean, however, that it fails to inform the whole existence of him who experiences it. On the contrary, as has been said in chapter 3, the person who achieves the deliverance of *nibbāna* thanks to the experience of insight lives in a specifically different mode. Even the most common activities or ordinary events are experienced and dealt with by him in ways which are different from those of the rest of us, conditioned as we are by countless desires, aversions and delusions. This is why, in the course of this book, I have repeatedly referred to the achievement of insight in terms of total integration, restructuring of the human psyche, and lasting transmutation of our usual intellectual and affective habits. Of course, all such terms are also only manners of speaking, generalities, but they attempt the only thing that can be attempted, which is to give an idea of the tremendously positive nature of the *nibbānic* state or experience, a state which (as was explained at the end of chapter 3) may be described as a higher state of consciousness, and which is distinguished by an attitude of total availability and openness towards one's fellow beings, in the fullness of the four cardinal virtues of Buddhism: compassion, sympathetic joy, loving kindness (or universal love) and perfect equanimity (which is the essential foundation of the other three). I shall come back to these virtues, or sublime states as they are called in traditional terminology, in the next chapter. Before that, however, I should like to close these brief comments on *nibbāna* by quoting three of the modern students of Buddhism who have best apprehended and formulated its vital significance:[205]

Its sentimental value to the exuberant optimism of the early Buddhists is one of peace and rest, perfect passionlessness, and thus supreme happiness [T. W. Rhys Davids].

Only by its concept is Nirvāṇa something negative; by its sentiment, however, it is a positive item in most pronounced form [R. Otto].

[*Nibbāna*] is a state of fulfilment, in which all needs and emotions have gone, a state of calm contentment and of complete intellectual insight. It is a state of internal freedom, where all dependence, insecurity and defence have disappeared. Ethical behaviour has become second nature, and the attitude towards others is friendliness, acceptance and humility [Rune Johansson].

8
Loving Kindness and Equanimity

1 In chapter 4 (section 4.6) a brief description was given of the use of the four sublime states as meditation subjects for the development of concentration. In chapter 5, when discussing tranquillity meditation, it was explained that three of these sublime states – loving kindness, compassion and sympathetic joy – may be used to achieve the third absorption, while equanimity is particularly suitable as a basis for the fourth absorption, which is distinguished by the predominance of precisely this quality. This covered the uses of the four sublime states as what we might call technical elements, for the cultivation of concentration to achieve certain stages in the development of tranquillity. But, as was already pointed out at the time, the truly important point about these sublime states, which may well be called the four cardinal virtues of Buddhism, is that they have a fundamental function in the moral and spiritual development of the meditator, which is important, not only for the development of tranquillity but, above all, for the progressive achievement of insight.

It is now time to say something about this aspect, and I shall do so with specific reference to two of the four sublime states, namely loving kindness and equanimity. There is no need at this point to enter into a separate discussion of the other two because (as already pointed out in chapter 4) loving kindness, or *mettā*, being the fullest manifestation of disinterested love for one's fellow beings, encompasses in itself both compassion and sympathetic joy (which are its specific manifestations in relation to the sufferings and the joys of others). Thus, what may be said about the former applies equally to the latter. As regards *upek-khā*, equanimity, a moment's reflection is enough to show its capital importance: a balanced frame of mind, untroubled by attachment or aversion, is the only possible root of truly disinterested love, of real altruism. Let us, therefore, take it first.

2 *Equanimity* (upekkhā)

As indicated in chapter 4, equanimity is part both of the means to liberation and of its end manifestations. Its function as part of the means was already seen in discussing the use of the sublime states as meditation subjects to develop mental concentration. In chapter 4 it was explained how, after the preliminary consideration (which, in the case of equanimity, relates to the harmfulness of emotion and the benefits of an even, peaceful mind), equanimity is cultivated in relation to different categories of persons with whom we have varying degrees of affective involvement, beginning with someone towards whom we harbour merely neutral feelings (where it is easiest to establish and maintain equanimity), then moving on to a loved person, and finally (which is the most difficult stage) developing equanimity towards someone with whom we are on hostile terms. In this case, the cultivation of equanimity pursues two purposes. First, in the development of tranquillity (i.e. in *samatha* meditation) it is a means for entering into, and dwelling in, the fourth absorption, which has equanimity, together with purity of mindfulness, as its essential factor. Secondly, it has a clear relevance to one's daily life, since it is obvious that the intensive experience of equanimity during the state of absorption (even though it does not produce the irreversible transformation of the psyche which can be achieved through insight meditation) does not fail to have a generally beneficial effect on the mental and emotional balance of the practitioner, even after he has come out of the absorption and returned to a 'normal' state of consciousness. This is especially the case if, on the basis of the absorption, the meditator has practised the exercise of 'extension', in which equanimity is cultivated, no longer in respect of specific individuals but extended to all living beings. This is a gradual extension of the equanimous awareness that has been developed, pervading all directions of space in equal measure and relating to all beings that may be found therein. A more detailed description of the 'extension' exercise (which is similar for all four sublime states) will be given shortly in connection with the cultivation of loving kindness. It is more appropriate to dwell on it in that connection because, in its less intensive form (i.e. based on access concentration rather than fully fixed concentration), *mettā* meditation, or meditation of loving kindness, representing both the cultivation and the manifestation of a selflessly loving frame of mind, is one of the most frequent and popular practices in traditionally Buddhist countries.

In regard to the final purpose, it must be borne in mind that equanimity is an integral element of the experience of *nibbāna*, since the higher state of consciousness that is the *nibbānic* state involves, among other attainments, the fullness and perfection of equanimity. Recalling that the ultimate achievement is the fruit of insight developed through *vipassanā* meditation, one can easily appreciate the close connection between equanimity and the progress of insight. This should also be clear from what has been said so far on the subject; in chapter 6, for instance, the essential importance was repeatedly stressed of maintaining at all times a non-reactive equanimous attitude in practising the observation of bodily and mental phenomena. Thus, equanimity is both a means of progress and, through gradual achievement, an increasingly perfected end. This is so because the direct knowledge of the impermanent and impersonal nature of all processes (and the accompanying realization of the fact that the cause of suffering lies in the ignorance, i.e. incorrect perception, which makes us cling to what must necessarily run through our fingers), being experienced as a positive deliverance from attachment, is clearly itself an experience of equanimity. The *arahant*, the fully realized human being, is characterized by an unshakable balance of mind and by the total openness and availability to others which are its corollaries.

3 Loving Kindness (mettā)

Loving kindness as a meditation subject for the development of concentration leading to the first three absorptions of tranquillity meditation has already been discussed in chapters 4 and 5. In addition, however, as has just been pointed out in connection with equanimity, the sublime states may be further developed through the exercise known as 'extension'. Here the meditator, starting either from the level of fixed concentration or from that of access concentration, uses the energy of the mind thus concentrated to pervade his environment, to an increasingly wider extent, with the sublime state that he has originally developed in himself. The method is similar to that adopted for 'extending the sign' described in chapter 5 (section 2.2.2), and the *Visuddhi Magga* resorts again to the same simile of a ploughman to describe it:

Just as a skilled ploughman first delimits an area and then does his ploughing, so first a single dwelling [normally the one where the meditator is at that time] should be delimited and loving-kindness developed towards all beings there, with the thought: 'May all beings in this dwelling be free from enmity, may they be happy . . .' and so on. When his mind has become supple and wieldy with respect to that, he can then delimit two dwellings. Next he can successively delimit three, four, five, six, seven, eight, nine, ten dwellings, one street, half the village, the whole village, the district, the kingdom, one direction (and another) and so on up to one world sphere, or even beyond that, and develop loving kindness towards the beings in such areas.[206]

This is not the only formula for the extension of loving kindness to pervade one's surroundings and even remoter areas. In fact, anyone can develop, along similar lines, a thought sequence to suit himself, since the words or concepts used (such as 'dwelling', 'street', etc.) serve simply to direct the mind towards specific areas and situations, so as to focus the flow of benevolent mental energy and avoid the mere sentimentality of vague good intentions without a definite aim. One or two other classic formulations will serve to illustrate the procedure further. There is one, for instance, where the meditator proceeds by categories of beings, rather than by spatial pervasion:

May all women be free from enmity, affliction and anxiety, may they be happy! May all men . . . , all those progressing towards enlightenment . . . , all those not progressing towards enlightenment . . . , all beings in states of bliss . . . , all human beings . . . , all beings in states of misery . . . , be free from enmity, affliction and anxiety, may they be happy![207]

Another very common *mettā* meditation is the pervasion of the ten directions of space (i.e. the four cardinal points, the four intermediate points, plus above and below). This is best performed following immediately upon a sitting of tranquillity or of insight meditation, to take advantage of the calm, concentrated state of mind. Here, the meditator generates and develops in himself thoughts of loving kindness towards all beings, until he feels permeated by loving kindness, and he then radiates those loving thoughts of boundless goodwill towards all beings in all directions, thus: 'May all beings to the East . . . , to the West . . . [and so on] be free from enmity, affliction and anxiety, may they be happy!'[208]

One of the most beautiful and characteristic loving-kindness meditations is found in a famous discourse of the Buddha on the subject, the *Discourse on the Practice of Loving Kindness (Karanīyamettāsutta)*:[209]

May all beings be happy,
whatever their living nature.
Whether weak or strong, omitting none,

whether long or large,
middle-sized or short, fine or coarse;
those which can be seen and those which cannot,
those that are near and those that are far,
those already born, and those that are to be,
may all beings be happy!
Let none another deceive,
nor despise anyone on any grounds,
nor with anger or thoughts of hate
let beings ever wish one another harm.
Just as a mother will give her life
to protect her one and only child,
just so towards all beings
should one boundlessly open one's mind.
With loving kindness towards the whole word
should one boundlessly open one's mind,
above, below and all around,
free from narrowness, ill will or hate.

Like equanimity, and for the same reasons, loving kindness is both a means to, and an end result of, realization. In tranquillity meditation its function as a means is more to the forefront, while in insight meditation the pure, disinterested love towards all beings is the natural expression of the level of experiential understanding and realization achieved by the meditator. The supreme example of this is, of course, the Buddha's own decision, after his own Enlightenment, to help others towards the same achievement, and the totally selfless manner in which he dedicated the next forty years of his life to teach to others what he had learned, for the good of all beings. A decision which each one of us can try to emulate by developing, as far as we can, the qualities described in soberly eloquent terms in the *Visuddhi Magga* when relating the attitude and behaviour of those 'great beings' who have achieved full enlightenment, i.e. the *arahants*:

For the well-stilled minds of great beings, wishing the good of all beings, not wishing beings to suffer, desiring the successful attainments of beings to endure, cultivating impartiality towards all beings, do not discriminate thus: 'To this one should be given, to that one should not be given.' They give gifts to all beings, which are a source of happiness. And in order to avoid doing harm to beings, they undertake the precepts of virtue. In order to perfect virtue, they practise renunciation. To avoid confusion as to what is good and what is bad for beings, they cleanse their understanding. They are ever energetic for the sake of the welfare and happiness of beings. Having acquired heroic fortitude through supreme energy, they are patient with beings' many kinds of faults. When they promise: 'We shall give you this, we shall do that for you,' they do not deceive. They are unshakably resolute upon the welfare and happiness of beings. With unshakable loving-kindness they place them first [i.e. before themselves]. Being equanimous, they expect no reward.[210]

9
The Practice of Vipassanā Today

1 Since the beginning of the twentieth century the teaching and the practice of traditional Buddhist meditation have undergone a considerable evolution in two important respects. First, there has been a decided growth in the practice of *vipassanā* meditation on its own (using perceptual exercises[211]), without combining it with *samatha* meditation, as used to be done in the past. That is to say, there has been a focusing on the direct pursuit of essential insight, without associating it with the methodical practice of tranquillity. Secondly, there has been a much greater involvement of lay persons in *vipassanā*, not only as students in ever growing numbers but also as lay meditation masters. Both these developments are mutually interrelated and are manifestations of the same overall trend: an adaptation to the conditions prevailing in the modern world, and a response to the growing demand for these simple and effective methods of mental culture.

Traditionally, Buddhist meditation used to be something practised in the well-regulated, supportive environment of a monastic retreat. The masters were always monks, and the great majority of regular disciples were also monks and nuns. Also (as was explained in chapter 3), disciples traditionally learned and practised not only *vipassanā* to achieve insight but also *samatha* to develop tranquillity. The reason for associating both techniques is very simple: the abstractive practices of tranquillity meditation, requiring as they do very high levels of mental concentration and producing the positive altered states of consciousness that have been described, are an excellent way of learning to control and develop the mind, rendering it thus fitter for the thorough pursuit of insight. The point has been most aptly made by the Venerable Nyānaponika:

125

In the Absorptions, the mind attains a very high degree of concentration, purity and calm, and reaches deep down into the subconscious sources of intuition. With such a preparation, the subsequent period of Insight-practice is likely to bring quicker and steadier results.[212]

However, the problem with *samatha* meditation is that – except in the comparatively infrequent cases of people who are exceptionally gifted in that direction – one needs, in order to make significant progress, quite a lot of time, freedom from disturbances, and a calm, collected setting. A monk's or a hermit's life has no shortage of these – rather, they are its essential conditions – but a lay person, on the other hand, has more often than not considerable difficulty in establishing and maintaining a reasonably supportive environment. In our time of high-speed living, countless distractions and increasingly complex problems, even the conditions of a monk's life may sometimes be less than ideal. This is why nowadays, while the traditional practice of combining both types of meditation is continued in many Buddhist monasteries, there has been a quite remarkable growth in the practice of pure *vipassanā* meditation in many quarters; it is better suited to our times and less difficult to reconcile with the constraints of a lay life.

The growing numbers of lay persons who seriously take up the practice of *vipassanā* is a typically modern phenomenon but one which is solidly rooted in ancient tradition. In fact, from the very beginning the Buddha addressed his teaching not only to yogis, recluses and monks, but also to lay persons in all walks of life, from kings and princes to merchants, farmers and barbers, from millionaires' wives and ordinary housewives to prostitutes. In the *Discourses* we see time and again how, as soon as he got to a town or village, the local population would come to listen to his teaching and to learn meditation (the first thing he taught them being usually mindfulness of breathing). A proportion of those, of course, were moved to leave the household life and become monks, but many instances are also recounted of people attaining one of the four levels of insight achievement (including the full enlightenment of an *arahant*)[213] without ever having left the secular state. Also, it has always been customary in Buddhist countries for lay persons to observe the main religious festivals (such as the full-moon day of May, the most important occasion in the Buddhist calendar, on which the birth, the enlightenment and the *parinibbāna*[214] of the Buddha are celebrated) by repairing to the nearest monastery, not only to attend the various ceremonies but also to practise retreats of shorter or longer duration (including temporary vows of chastity, abstinence, etc.), during which they train in insight meditation. There is even more: in a country such as Thailand, it is to this day an established custom for teenagers, or even for children, to spend a period of three months or more as temporary novices in a monastery, as part of the normal social and educational process of growing up, following exactly the same moral and mental discipline, including meditation, of *sāmaneras*, i.e. the longer-term novices who are preparing for a full monk's ordination.

All this illustrates the point made at the beginning of this book that the practice of meditation is the heart of the Buddha's teaching, and it is within this context that the modern growth of *vipassanā* practice by lay persons must be understood. This developed particularly in Burma in the early part of the century and has spread vigorously since then, first to other countries in Asia and then also to Europe, America and Australia.

In the latter part of this chapter I shall present this 'lay current' by describing the methods of U Ba Khin, its foremost exponent, who was also a high government official in Burma, and of his successor S. N. Goenka, a business magnate turned meditation master. Before that, however, it will be useful to consider *vipassanā* meditation as taught in our days still within the monastic tradition by another leading meditation master, the Venerable Mahāsi Sayadaw. As the head of Thathana Yeiktha, the great meditation centre in Rangoon, he was concerned not only with teaching other monks but also many lay persons, including numerous Westerners, and was thus one of the main sources for the spread of *vipassanā* in the world of today.[215]

2 *The Monk Mahāsi Sayadaw (1904–82)*

2.1 *The Man*

Before becoming a leading meditation master, the Venerable Mahāsi Sayadaw was already known as a learned scholar and teacher of the Pali scriptures. Born in a rural district, at the age of six he began attending the local monastery school in his native village, and at the age of twelve he was ordained as a novice. He became a monk on reaching the age of twenty, the earliest age at which full ordination is possible, with the name of Sobhana (which was his ordained monastic name, while Mahāsi Sayadaw is simply a honorific title, by which, however, he became universally known). In the following years he pursued higher Pali and Buddhist studies, attained the highest scholastic distinctions and devoted himself for some time to the teaching of these subjects.

The day came, however, at the age of twenty-eight, when he felt the powerful need to move on from the sphere of intellectual understanding and exposition to that of intensive practice. Accordingly, taking up the bare requisites of a wandering monk's life (essentially, the almsbowl and a set of robes), he left the renowned monastery where he had been teaching and set out, like one of the early disciples of the Buddha, in search of a master who would train him in a clear and effective method for the practice of meditation. He found him in the person of the Venerable Mingun Jetawan Sayadaw (U Nārada Mahāthera, 1868–1955), recognized as the fountainhead of the renewed use in modern times of the ancient techniques of the four foundations of mindfulness (as described in chapter 6) for the practice of insight meditation, i.e. *vipassanā*. In this connection I can do no better than quote what the Venerable Nyānaponika has written in *The Heart of Buddhist Meditation*:

It was at the beginning of this century that a Burmese monk, U Nārada by name, bent on actual realization of the teachings he had learnt, was eagerly searching for a system of meditation offering a direct access to the Highest Goal, without encumbrance by accessories. Wandering through the country, he met many who were given to strict meditative practice, but he could not obtain guidance satisfactory to him. In the course of his quest, coming to the famous meditation-caves in the hills of Sagaing in Upper Burma, he met a monk who was reputed to have entered upon those lofty Paths of Sanctitude [i.e. the stages of purification described in chapter 6, section 2.6.1 above] where the final achievement of liberation is assured. When the Venerable U Nārada put his question to him, he was asked in return: 'Why are you searching outside the Master's word? Has not the Only Way, Satipatthāna, been proclaimed by Him?' U Nārada took up this indication. Studying again the text and its traditional exposition, reflecting deeply on it, and entering energetically upon its practice, he finally came to understand its salient features. The results achieved in his own practice convinced him that he had found what he was searching for: a clear-cut and effective method of training the mind for highest realization. From his own experience he developed the principles and the details of the practice which formed the basis for those who followed him as his direct or indirect disciples. . . . He passed away on the 18th March 1955, aged 87. Many believe that he attained to final deliverance (Arahatta).[216]

Under the guidance of this highly competent master, Mahāsi Sayadaw undertook intensive meditation training based on the four foundations of mindfulness, beginning with the contemplation of the body, and made considerable progress. After this, without neglecting the practice of *vipassanā*, he went back to his learned studies and teaching activities, gaining increasing recognition as a scholar of highest standing. In 1941, in the eighteenth year of his ordination, he decided to return to his native village, where he took up residence in a local monastery and began teaching systematic practical courses of *vipassanā* meditation on the basis of the foundations of mindfulness.

Many people, lay persons as well as monks, came to his courses and benefited from his instruction. He soon became well known throughout the country as a very effective teacher of insight meditation. So much so, in fact, that in 1949 – shortly after Burma's independence – U Nu, the first Prime Minister of the country, requested the Venerable Mahāsi Sayadaw to come to Rangoon to teach intensive training courses at Thathana Yeiktha, the headquarters of the National Buddhist Association. From that time, and until the death of Mahāsi Sayadaw at the age of seventy-eight, in 1982, many thousands of persons have learned insight meditation at the Rangoon centre (by 1973 over 15,000 students had already passed through there) and literally hundreds of thousands have been instructed in over a hundred local centres throughout Burma, under the guidance of teachers trained by Mahāsi Sayadaw himself. Outside Burma, similar centres exist in Sri Lanka, India and Thailand.

In recognition of his outstanding achievements as a scholar, teacher and meditation master, Mahāsi Sayadaw was appointed to the key position of 'Questioner' at the Sixth Buddhist Council held in Rangoon from 1954 to 1956 in celebration of the 2500th anniversary of the proclamation of the Buddha's teaching. The Questioner plays an extremely responsible role in a Buddhist Council, since it is he who has to raise all the questions of substance or of form which may be relevant in the course of the complete review of the scriptures carried out at each Council.

2.2 The Method[217]

2.2.1 Introduction

Mahāsi Sayadaw's meditation method, as learned by him from Mingun Sayadaw, is based, as already mentioned, on the four foundations of mindfulness (*satipaṭṭhāna*) and takes the contemplation of the body as its primary subject. Traditionally, the meditation subject most commonly used for the contemplation of the body has always been the first one mentioned in the discourse, i.e. the mindfulness of breathing (as was seen in chapter 6). Mahāsi Sayadaw, however, introduced a variant form of the exercise. Having noticed that there were people who had difficulty in perceiving the relatively light sensations connected with the breath in the nostrils and on the upper lip, he decided to resort to another one of the traditional body contemplation exercises, namely the third one of the series as it appears in the discourse, i.e. the exercise of 'clear comprehension

129

of every action' (see chapter 6, section 2.2.3). The basis of Mahāsi Sayadaw's method is, therefore, this exercise which involves maintaining a constant awareness, moment by moment, of whatever one is doing or experiencing. However, it is rather difficult, especially for a beginner, to achieve the initial concentration necessary for successful practice if one has to start straight away by paying close attention to *every* action. It was therefore necessary to select some particular aspect of bodily activity as a primary subject to start practice on. For this purpose, and on the basis of his own practice and of his experience with his students, Mahāsi Sayadaw decided to begin by focusing attention on a bodily movement which is intimately related with the act of breathing (thus linking up with the traditional mindfulness of breathing exercise) and which, like the breath itself, is both automatic and amenable to voluntary control. This is the movement of the abdomen resulting from the process of breathing. In fact, even though we do not normally pay attention to it, our abdomen expands every time we breathe in and contracts every time we breathe out – the 'rising and falling of the abdomen' as Mahāsi Sayadaw put it. Although this rising and falling is part of the muscular processes necessarily involved in the act of breathing, it is not to be regarded as identical with 'mindfulness of breathing', but rather as a direct focusing on a bodily process in the specific sense of the exercise of 'clear comprehension of every action.'

Let us now see the outline of an insight meditation course as conducted at Thathana Yeiktha and other centres following the Burmese method of Mahāsi Sayadaw. The courses last normally one or two months and are of a highly intensive character. Up to sixteen hours a day are devoted to meditation, alternating periods of sitting meditation and walking meditation (as described in chapter 6, section 2.2.2.2), and maintaining in addition the maximum possible degree of conscious awareness in all actions performed while attending to the daily necessities of life, outside the periods of formal meditation. The basic course comprises a preparatory stage and four basic exercises, combined with a certain amount of walking meditation.

2.2.2 *Preparatory Stage*

2.2.2.1 *The Eight Precepts*

First of all, the new student is asked, for the duration of the course, to follow the discipline of the eight precepts observed by lay persons in Buddhist countries on religious festivals and during meditation retreats.

The eight precepts require one to abstain from: (1) destroying any living being (even, for instance, a mosquito that may be bothering one), (2) stealing, (3) any kind of sexual activity, (4) lying, (5) intoxicants, (6) partaking of solid food after twelve noon (although certain liquids, such as fruit juices or tea, are permitted in the afternoon), (7) dancing, attending or performing in shows or entertainments, using perfumes, cosmetics, personal ornaments, etc., (8) using high or luxurious beds (this is the traditional phrase – the meaning is to abstain from using excessively comfortable or luxurious furniture).

2.2.2.2 *The Four Protections*

Secondly, it is suggested that, for the duration of the course, one should mentally place oneself under the protection of the Buddha and the guidance of the meditation instructor. There is a practical reason for this, namely that, depending on the student's mental condition, experiences or visions may arise which can cause fear, anxiety, confusion, etc., and in such cases it is an excellent psychological protection to have placed one's trust entirely not only in the qualified instructor with whom one is working but also in the great master himself, the Buddha, who personally developed and perfected in all its essential aspects the technique that one is oneself learning.

Thereupon the student is asked to engage in a brief contemplation of the traditional 'four protections', based on four of the recollections described in chapter 4, namely: the Buddha (section 4.3.1), loving kindness (4.6.1), the repulsiveness of the body (4.3.9.4 and 4.3.9.7, and also chapter 6, 2.2.4), and death (4.3.7). Here the recollections are normally carried out with only a mild degree of mental concentration (preparatory concentration, as described in chapter 4, section 1.1), reflecting on each one of the subjects on the basis of the formulas already mentioned (in the case of loving kindness, one cultivates goodwill towards all beings along the lines described in chapter 8, section 3, at a simple discursive level). These preliminary contemplations are referred to as 'protections' because their purpose is to ensure the psychological safety of the practitioner through his cultivating a confident, detached and positive frame of mind.

2.2.3 *Basic Exercise I*

One takes up a sitting posture, with legs crossed, a straight back, and the hands resting in one's lap. (Alternative ways of sitting may be resorted to if one cannot manage a traditional crosslegged posture.) The eyes may be slightly open, but not focused on anything in particular, allowing one's glance to fall naturally, according to the position of the head. (Unlike other methods, here one does not work with visual contemplation; the eyes could be entirely closed, but keeping them half open helps to prevent drowsiness, especially in beginners.)

The instruction is as follows:

Try to keep your mind (but not your eyes) on the abdomen. You will thereby come to know the movements of rising and falling of this organ. If these movements are not clear to you in the beginning, then place both hands on the abdomen to feel these rising and falling movements. After a short time, the upward movement of inhalation [expansion] and the downward movement of exhalation [contraction] will become clear. Then make a mental note, *rising* for the upward movement, and *falling* for the downward movement. Your mental note of each movement must be made while it occurs.[218]

That is all at this stage. But it is already quite a lot: to keep one's attention constantly focused on the observed process is far from easy when one is not used to it. It is important, however, to persevere, bearing always in mind that the purpose is to maintain pure perceptual observation, as free as possible from mental and affective associations (ideas, reflections, emotions, moods, etc.). The instruction to 'make a mental note' of each movement as *rising* or *falling* is simply to explain what it is exactly that should be observed, but one should never verbally repeat the words 'rising', 'falling', nor think of 'rising' and 'falling' as words. There should be nothing but an increasingly clear awareness of the actual process of the rising and falling movement of the abdomen, without mental 'background noise'. Nor should the breathing process be interfered with (by deliberate deep or rapid breathing) in order to make the abdominal movements more distinct. Like all *vipassanā* practice, this is an exercise in observation and any manipulation, no matter how well meant, is an interference.

2.2.4 *Basic Exercise II*

In spite of one's determination to focus on nothing but each one of the abdominal movements, other mental activities may occur (and, in the case of a beginner, they will almost certainly do so) between the noting of each rising and falling: thoughts, volitions, fancies, etc., are likely to arise and must not be disregarded. The way to deal with them is to make a mental note of each one *as it occurs*.

The instruction here is:

If you imagine something, you must know that you have done so, and make a mental note *imagining*. If you simply think of something, mentally note *thinking*. If you reflect, *reflecting*. If you intend to do something, *intending*. When the mind wanders from the object of meditation, which is the rising and falling of the abdomen, mentally note *wandering*. . . . If you envision and imagine a light or colour, be sure to note *seeing*. A mental vision must be noted on each occurrence of its appearance, until it passes away.[219]

The same procedure is applied to any physical action performed during the meditation session, such as swallowing saliva, bending or straightening one's back, etc. In these cases, however, it is important to note also the preliminary intention, i.e. when intending to swallow saliva, make a mental note *intending*, and while actually swallowing, note *swallowing*, and similarly for all other actions. Any bodily movements or adjustments of the body's position should be performed slowly and deliberately, and in each case, after mentally making a note of each intention and of each action, the practitioner carries on with noticing the movements of the rising and falling abdomen.

2.2.5 *Basic Exercise III*

Since the meditative position has to be maintained for long periods, it is natural that sensations of fatigue, stiffness in the body or in the extremities, itches, aches and pains, etc., may arise. When this happens, the focus of attention should be directed to the part of the body where the sensation occurs, and the contemplation carried on by noting *tired*, *stiff*, *itchy*, or whatever, without reacting, just as is done with the abdominal movements. Normally, these sensations, when they are subjected to detached observation (i.e. without identifying with them) gradually become fainter and finally cease altogether. When this has occurred, one should deliberately turn one's attention back to the abdominal movements. However, should one of these sensations, as can sometimes happen, become more intense until the bodily fatigue or stiffness becomes unbearable, then one may change one's position. In such a case, however, it is absolutely essential that both the intention and every stage of the movement should be clearly noted with full awareness. If, for instance, one needs to stretch a leg and fold it again in some other position, one should mentally note each phase as *intending* . . . *unfolding* . . . *stretching* . . . *folding* . . . *touching* (the ground) . . . *resting* (in the new position), and then proceed with the observation of the rising and falling of the abdomen. It is even permissible to lie down from time to time, provided that this is done quite deliberately and that, as soon as one is lying down, one proceeds with the contemplation of *rising* and *falling*

133

of the abdomen and that at the slightest sign of drowsiness one goes back to a sitting position or changes to walking meditation.

The same method should be applied to all mental events occurring during the practice, that is to say that one should immediately note every thought, intention, emotion, fantasy, etc., that may arise at the very moment it arises. But without going into detail, i.e. simply noting *thinking, intending, emoting, imagining,* and so on.

This attitude of constant vigilance and attention should be maintained not only during the periods of formal sitting meditation but throughout the day, from the moment one wakes up in the morning until going to bed at night. On awakening, one should immediately focus on the rising and falling of the abdomen. When getting out of bed, every one of the necessary movements should be performed mindfully, e.g. pushing back the bedclothes, sitting up in bed, swinging one's legs over the edge, placing one's feet on the ground, standing up, etc. And one should go on like this throughout the day, paying close, mindful attention to everything one does, while washing or taking a bath, while dressing, eating (i.e. sitting down at table, looking at the food, stretching out one's hand, taking a morsel, placing it in one's mouth, feeling the contact of the morsel on one's lips, on the tongue and palate, chewing, tasting, swallowing, etc.), while walking to the meditation hall, sitting down, beginning to contemplate the abdominal movements. And so on in this manner until one goes to bed at night, paying close attention to every action involved in preparing for bed, lying down, covering oneself with the bedclothes, etc., and then back to observing the abdominal movements, and mindfully noting increasing drowsiness until one falls asleep.

This is, fundamentally, a body contemplation exercise based on the sense of touch, and it is therefore recommended to ignore visual or auditory stimuli. However, if certain sounds or sights are powerful enough to intrude, one should deal with them as with all other occurrences, i.e. turn deliberately to them for a moment and make a mental note *seeing, hearing,* and then return to the rising and falling of the abdomen.

In short, during every moment of one's waking hours, day or night, one should be fully aware and mindful of every action, thought or feeling, and whenever there is nothing in particular to observe one should revert to contemplating the abdominal movements of rising and falling. This is the full practice of the exercise of 'clear comprehension of every action', with a primary subject, i.e. the rising and falling of the abdomen, as an ever present basis.

2.2.6 *Walking Meditation during Intervals*

In between periods of sitting meditation one may engage in mindful walking, or walking meditation, which provides some variety and helps relieve the numbness or stiffness of the body without interrupting mental concentration (see the description of this kind of meditation practice in chapter 6). In addition, throughout the day, whenever one has to move from one place to another, for instance from the meditation hall to the refectory, one should always walk mindfully, i.e. being fully aware of the movement, at least in three stages (*lifting . . . forward . . . lowering and putting down*) or in two (*lifting and forward . . . lowering and putting down*).

2.2.7 *Basic Exercise IV*

In Basic Exercise II it was explained that, during sitting meditation using the abdominal movements as the primary perceptual input, the practitioner should maintain full awareness of whatever mental events occur as a means of ensuring the continuity of deliberate, mindful observation. In Basic Exercise IV this attitude of continuous, unbroken mindfulness is extended to cover everything that arises in the psyche throughout the day – all mental, volitive and affective processes. For instance, if one feels pleased at one's progress, one should immediately make a mental note *pleased*, if one feels discouraged, note *discouraged*, if one is mentally reviewing the instructions to ensure correct practice, note *reviewing*, if one is analysing a certain sensation or occurrence, note *analysing*, and so on. The essential point, which cannot be sufficiently stressed, is that throughout the day and any waking hours of the night, attention should be constantly exercised in a deliberate and fully conscious manner, noting at all times whatever is occurring in the body and in the mind *as it occurs*, and whenever nothing in particular presents itself returning to the rising and falling of the abdomen.

2.2.8 *Conclusion*

This, briefly outlined, is the method. The subdivision into four basic exercises is purely methodological, to make it easier to explain things to a new student and to guide his first attempts, since one has to start somewhere. It is quite clear, however, that these four exercises are not alternatives (except in the mechanical sense that while sitting one is not walking or lying down, and so on) but mutually complementary and progressive in scope. From the very beginning, as soon as the meditator achieves a degree of firm focusing of attention, he is already (to the extent of his ability at that time) paying attention to whatever is occurring as it occurs. And it is in this way that he begins to perceive, through his own direct experience, the transience of all phenomena, and to develop insight into their impermanent and impersonal nature.

3 *The Lay Master U Ba Khin (1899–1971)*

3.1 *The Man*

U Ba Khin, recognized as one of the greatest meditation masters of our time and an energetic promoter of the lay tradition (as distinct from the monastic one) of insight meditation practice, was one of those powerful figures who make a success of everything they undertake. Born in Rangoon in modest circumstances, he displayed considerable intellectual ability from an early age, gained scholarships and was thus able to obtain a good education, including the knowledge of English that was essential to advancement at that time when Burma was under British rule. He started his career in public service as an accounts clerk in the Accountant General's Office for Burma, at a time when only very few Burmese managed to enter the service. His subsequent career was highly successful. Under British rule he was successively promoted to posts of increasing responsibility, including, in 1937, that of Special Office Superintendent in the then newly established Office of the Auditor General of Burma. As soon as Burma gained its independence, in January 1948, he was immediately appointed Accountant General, a post of particularly delicate responsibility in a newly independent nation. He retired from that position in 1953 (which, at the age of fifty-five, may seem early by current Western standards, but was normal at the time in a tropical country and in accordance with the conditions inherited from the British Colonial Service). However, he was not able to devote himself full time to the teaching of meditation, as he might have hoped. In fact, owing to the scarcity of highly qualified personnel which is so acutely felt in Third World countries, he was immediately requested to re-enter public service in a variety of other highly responsible capacities and found himself even busier than before. At various times – and, most of the time, simultaneously – he held the posts (at head of government department level) of Director of Commercial Audit, Chairman of the State Agricultural Marketing Board and founding Principal of the Government Institute for Accounts and Audit (established in order to train qualified accounting staff). In addition, he was frequently called upon to chair various government boards and committees, including the chairmanship of the Standing Committee for National Planning, an ad hoc committee on the reorganization of the civil service, and many others.

Alongside these manifold professional activities, U Ba Khin led an equally full personal life – he married young and had six children – and he does not seem to have ever felt that there was any incompatibility between professional and household life on the one hand and, on the other, the practice and – to an increasing extent – the teaching of *vipassanā* meditation. On the contrary, he always used to say that Buddhist meditation 'is a reservoir of calm and balanced energy', from which he himself seems to have drawn inexhaustible energy ever since he began practising it.

U Ba Khin started *vipassanā* meditation in 1937. His first contact with the technique was when he was encouraged to try mindfulness of breathing by a house guest who was a student of Saya Thet Gyi, a pioneer lay teacher of the technique. Saya Thet Gyi was a well-to-do farmer who, having discovered in himself a great inclination to insight meditation, spent many years studying and practising it under one of the famous teaching monks, the Venerable Ledi Sayadaw (1846–1923). In due course Saya Thet Gyi was declared fully proficient by Ledi Sayadaw and authorized to teach *vipassanā* as a lay meditation master. As his fame spread, more and more lay persons started coming to him for instruction. They were ordinary people, who did not intend to give up the household life for more than brief periods of training or temporary retreats, but who, having understood the great benefits of *vipassanā*, were keen to learn it properly and to practise it in their daily life. U Ba Khin was one of those. He made rapid progress during his first intensive ten-day course with Saya Thet Gyi, and continued for some years to work with his teacher during the latter's frequent visits to Rangoon.

U Ba Khin began to do some teaching himself in 1941, encouraged by a monk who had been impressed by his achievements. He imparted instruction to individuals and small groups as and when it could be fitted into his very busy professional schedule, but it was not until 1950 that he embarked on a more comprehensive scheme. He did so, characteristically, within the framework of his professional activities and for the benefit of those with whom he shared them. At that time he was the Accountant General of Burma, and the way he started was by offering meditation classes to those of his staff who showed an interest in them. He conducted sessions of mindfulness of breathing and of *vipassanā*, at the end of the day's work, first in his own office and later, as numbers increased, in a spare room which he reserved for this specific purpose in

137

the same building. Thus he founded, in July 1950, the Vipassanā Association of the Accountant General's Office, devoted to the teaching of meditation by and for lay persons.

As recalled by one of his early students (Saya U Tint Yee, now President of the International Meditation Centre in Rangoon), in those first years 'there were no full ten-day courses, and we meditated in our houses, and in the office meditation room before and after office hours'.[220] In view of constantly growing demand, however, the need for a properly organized centre where intensive courses (like those that used to be taught by Saya Thet Gyi) could be held in a suitable environment soon came to be keenly felt. Thus, as early as 1952, U Ba Khin, with the enthusiastic help of many supporters, founded the International Meditation Centre in Rangoon, an institution which has continued to flourish up to the present day. There he was able to start giving intensive ten-day courses on a regular basis, perfecting the 'total immersion' method for the benefit of lay people which has since become so widespread both in the East and in the West. Let us again turn to U Tint Yee's reminiscences:

After the pagoda was built [this being a domelike structure with individual cells where the students practise under the teacher's supervision] U Ba Khin started giving ten-day courses at the Centre. Every course started on the first Friday evening of each month, so that the office staff could join the course by taking only six days' leave [i.e. taking advantage of two weekends]. The families of the staff and their close friends were then given permission to join the courses if they wished.

It was also in that Centre that U Ba Khin gradually trained new teachers who helped him to instruct the growing numbers of students, and who are today keeping up his teaching tradition not only in Rangoon but in other parts of the world. Something will be said about them in a moment, in particular on S. N. Goenka, who has been the most powerfully active of them all, and whose basic ten-day course will be briefly described as an example of U Ba Khin's method in action. Before that, however, I should like to conclude this biographical sketch with a quotation from John Coleman, another one of the influential teachers trained by U Ba Khin, which sums up his personality admirably:

Here was a good man in the real sense of the word. A gentle, quietly spoken and humorous teacher of a faith which possessed the means of solving some of humanity's problems, but which above all was a personal faith which, followed devoutly and practised assiduously, could arm its adherents against the difficulties which life presents to the individual. . . . I came to know U Ba Khin as a simple teacher, a profound thinker, a lover of beauty. . . . I had found that, to him, beauty, compassion, spiritual peace, truth, morality and so on were not just words, nor were they an end in themselves. They were a way of life, part of his very existence.[221]

3.2 The Method

U Ba Khin's method is rooted in the same ancient tradition as Mahāsi Sayadaw's – being also based on the practice of the four foundations of mindfulness, with the contemplation of the body as primary subject – but it follows the tradition even more closely in that it uses the direct observation of the breath (rather than the related abdominal movements) to concentrate the mind, by starting with the exercise of mindfulness of breathing. A particular characteristic of U Ba Khin's method is the unremitting intensity of practice during short periods (the basic course lasting always only ten days) to provide a total immersion for people who can spare little time and have to go back at once to the multiple involvements of daily life. For this reason, too, U Ba Khin always stressed the practical, concrete aspects of meditation work, keeping theoretical or doctrinal explanations to a minimum. The point was, and is, to live the *Dhamma* through one's own experience (this being, of course, the essence of the Buddha's teaching), by applying a practical, direct and intensive method.

Briefly outlined, the method consists in concentrating the mind to begin with through the practice of mindfulness of breathing, and then turning the concentrated attention that has thus been achieved to the various parts of one's physical organism – moving systematically throughout the body – in order to develop an increasingly thorough and subtle awareness of all the sensations which arise in it. The purpose is to perceive with increasing clarity all sensations that occur, whatever they may be, including those which are normally below the threshold of everyday unconcentrated attention and – through this perception – to develop an increasingly full and penetrating awareness of the continual arising and passing away of physical and mental phenomena whose manifestations they are. This is, of course, the contemplation of the body and of sensations (the first two of the four foundations of mindfulness). At the same time, and similarly to Mahāsi Sayadaw's method, all thoughts, emotions, volitions, reflections, etc., which arise during the practice must be deliberately noted as soon as they occur, which is, in effect, an application of the other two foundations of mindfulness (contemplation of the mind and of mental contents), but only to the extent necessary to maintain unbroken continuity of attention. After briefly noting the thought, etc. (but without going so far as even to name it, unlike what is done in Mahāsi Sayadaw's technique), one returns at once to the contemplation of the body and of sensations, which is the essence of this method. As the Buddha said: 'It is in this very fathom-long body, with its perceptions and with its mind that I make known the world, and the arising of the world, and the extinction of the world, and the path leading to the extinction of the world.'[222]

As the perception of bodily processes grows finer and more precise, the meditator develops an increasing awareness of the fact that they are all unstable and transient. This is the experience of *anicca*, the radical impermanence of everything that exists. In U Ba Khin's terminology, this experience is described as 'activating *anicca*', and it is this activation, that is to say, the experiential awareness of impermanence, which – as it grows – gradually cleanses our psyche of the desires, clingings, hates, rejections, anxieties, fears, hopes, etc., with which we are constantly beset. This is what I have repeatedly referred to as a transmutation, or re-ordering, of the human psyche, whose effects extend also to the physical organism, often alleviating many psychosomatic conditions. U Ba Khin described the liberating mode of experience as *nibbāna dhātu*, which means literally '*nibbāna* element'. In its traditional sense this term is, to all practical purposes, a synonym of *nibbāna* pure and simple – when the scriptures speak about *nibbāna dhātu* they refer to the living experience of *nibbāna*. In U Ba Khin's usage the term highlights the dynamic process nature of *nibbānic* experience. As usual, we run here into the difficulty of trying to describe in conceptual terms something that cannot be apprehended in those terms. Very roughly, however, one might say that as the meditator penetrates more and more deeply into the real nature of phenomena through an increasingly clear awareness of *anicca*, that is to say, through an ever more penetrating insight into their impermanence, a time comes when there arises a distinct experiential mode or element (*dhātu*) which has the effect of eliminating those desires, hates and all the rest. To help one understand what is involved (and without implying thereby any exact correspondence with the terminology of Western psychology), one might say that, through a sort of process of abreaction, the psyche is gradually freed from the neuroses which, in effect, make up the tissue of what we like to call our personality. More particularly, the attachment to this 'personality' and to 'its' world is dissolved. 'In the same way as fuel is burnt away by ignition, the negative forces (impurities or poisons) within are eliminated by the *nibbāna dhātu*, which the student generates with the true awareness of *anicca* in the course of his meditation,' U Ba Khin used to say. And he stressed:

140

The experience of Anicca, when properly developed, strikes at the root of one's physical and mental ills and removes gradually whatever is bad in him, i.e. the causes of such physical and mental ills. This experience is not reserved for men who have renounced the world for the homeless life. It is for the householder as well. In spite of drawbacks which make a householder restless in these days, a competent teacher or guide can help a student to get the experience of Anicca activated in a comparatively short time. Once he has got it activated, all that is necessary is for him to try and preserve it.

And, of course, to develop it further, for which reason it is essential, after having completed a course, to keep up regular practice on one's own. U Ba Khin, however, being an eminently pragmatic person, did not expect a busy householder to do the impossible:

There is no need for him to be activating the experience of Anicca all the time. It should suffice if this could be confined to a regular period, or periods, set apart in the day or night for the purpose. During this time, at least, an attempt must be made to keep the attention focused inside the body, with awareness devoted exclusively to Anicca; that is to say, his awareness of Anicca should go on from moment to moment so continuously as not to allow for the interpolation of any discursive or distracting thoughts which are definitely detrimental to progress.

And, speaking with all the authority of his own experience, he concluded:

We have no doubt whatsoever that definite results would accrue to those who would with an open mind sincerely undergo a course of training under a competent teacher – I mean results which will be accepted as good, concrete, vivid, personal, here-and-now, results which will keep them in good stead and in a state of well-being and happiness for the rest of their lives.[223]

3.3 *The Successors*

In over thirty years since the International Meditation Centre was established in Rangoon, many people (both from Burma and other Buddhist countries in Asia, as well as many who came from Europe, America and Australia) have been able to experience there the benefits of *vipassanā* meditation. Some of them, who showed special aptitude and dedication, were given further training by U Ba Khin, to qualify them as fully competent lay teachers, and it is especially through them that the teaching of *vipassanā* has spread to other countries and continents. John Coleman, one of the early American followers of U Ba Khin who settled in England, has been teaching actively for many years both in Britain and on the European continent, as well as from time to time in North

America, and has been possibly the first to take the technique to Latin America. More recently the Burmese Mother Sayama (who for some years ran the International Meditation Centre in Rangoon after U Ba Khin's death) has also established herself in England. In America Ruth Denison and Robert Hover were the pioneers, and others have followed them in recent years in disseminating U Ba Khin's method. The most dynamic of these 'first generation' teachers, however, and the one who has had the greatest impact worldwide is, without doubt, the Indo-Burmese S. N. Goenka.

3.3.1 S. N. Goenka (b. 1924)

Satya Narayan Goenka was born in Burma into a well-to-do Indian family of the merchant class (part of the thriving community of Indian traders and businessmen who had settled in Burma under the British Raj), and brought up in the strict Hindu tradition. He enjoyed a good education, went into business – following the family vocation – and proved extremely successful. For years he led the very busy, demanding existence of a high-level business leader, involving much travel and manifold responsibilities. He married and raised a family, thus leading also a full personal life. This very active and full existence, however, did not make him forget the needs of those less fortunate than himself, and he always found time and energy to devote to social welfare and community service activities.

There was, however, another aspect to this by ordinary standards successful and happy life, and this was the fact that S. N. Goenka had suffered from childhood of extremely intense, sometimes temporarily disabling migraine, which no amount of medical care and attention (not only in Burma, but also in Western countries and in Japan) had managed to bring under control. He was in the end reduced to taking increasingly powerful painkillers, including morphine, and it was at that stage, at the age of thirty-one, that he was persuaded to try one of U Ba Khin's courses (having heard of other cases in which painful physical conditions had been relieved). Overcoming both his own hesitations (on account of his Hindu religious background) and his family's discouragement, in 1955 S. N. Goenka went to the renowned Buddhist lay master for a ten-day course. The impact of this first experience was a powerful one – not only in doing away with the illness which had troubled him for some twenty-five years (he has never suffered from migraine since), but also in giving him a glimpse of the deep insight that could be achieved into the nature of existence. Without abandoning his professional and household duties, he became from then on an assiduous student of U Ba Khin, and he spent the next fourteen years devoting himself, with characteristic energy, to the thorough learning and practice of *vipassanā*, also gradually assisting U Ba Khin in the running of the Centre in various capacities.

Meanwhile the political and economic climate in Burma was becoming increasingly unfavourable to private enterprise, and many members of the long-established Indian community there were endeavouring to return to their homeland. So it was, too, with S. N. Goenka's family. By 1969, S. N. Goenka himself obtained permission from the Burmese authorities to leave the country and return to India, where he had already been preceded by his parents and other members of his family. It was in Bombay, in that same year, that – as authorized by U Ba Khin – he conducted his first *vipassanā* course on his own. This was done for the benefit of his mother and a very small group of relatives and friends, no more than thirteen or fourteen persons in all. It quickly became obvious that there was a very urgent need for *vipassanā*. This first course was followed very soon by others, organized at the pressing request of those who had heard of the striking results of the practice, and within a short time S. N. Goenka was travelling all over India, called upon to teach *vipassanā* to increasingly larger groups. His 'camps' (as they were called during this first itinerant period) were attended by people of all races, social groups, faiths and personal and professional backgrounds.

The first permanent teaching centre came into being in 1976, with the establishment of the Vipassanā International Academy (VIA) in the small town of Igatpuri, in the State of Maharashtra, about three hours by train from Bombay. Since then two other centres have been established in India, in Jaipur and in Hyderabad, and smaller centres are being developed in Dharamsala (in the Himalayas), in Barachakia (State of Bihar) and in Nepal. In the West, a Vipassanā Meditation Center was inaugurated in the USA at Shelburne Falls (Massachusetts) in 1982, and other centres are being planned in Great Britain and in Australia.

At first S. N. Goenka had to combine his increasingly intensive teaching schedule with continued attention to professional and business matters. Some years ago, however, he was able to retire entirely from these so as to devote all his energies to teaching. Since then he has not only been teaching basic and more advanced courses to students but also training assistant teachers, who can help him meet the increasing demand for *vipassanā* in many parts of the world. He himself travels regularly every year, holding courses in Europe, the United States, Canada, Japan, Australia and New Zealand. In all his teaching work he has always been able to rely on the support and cooperation of his wife, who accompanies him on his travels and participates regularly in practice sessions and *Dhamma* talks.

Since the death of U Ba Khin in 1971, S. N. Goenka has been generally recognized as the main exponent of *vipassanā* training through intensive, total-immersion courses. These, as already explained, are basically aimed at lay persons who can only manage brief retreats and who go back immediately to their accustomed personal and professional lives. They are also, however, open to anyone else who may wish to attend. Over the years they have in fact attracted ordained religious of various persuasions, not only – as was to be expected – Buddhist monks but also Jains and Hindus, and a remarkably large number of Christian priests, monks and nuns, including some prominent personalities such as the Jesuit father Anthony de Melo, who has devoted a whole book, *Sadhāna*, to a detailed exposition of *vipassanā*, relating it to a Christian context.

I should now like to close this chapter and, with it, this presentation of the foundations of Buddhist meditation according to the oldest tradition, with a brief description of a basic intensive *vipassanā* course according to U Ba Khin's method. The purpose of this is twofold: first, to give the reader an idea of what is involved in taking part in a course, and secondly to stress again what was said at the beginning of this book, i.e. that theory without practice is of no real use – like giving a hungry person a cookery book instead of a plate of food.

3.3.2 *Intensive Courses*

3.3.2.1 *Preliminaries: Introduction and Discipline*

On registering, each participant is handed a leaflet containing an Introduction to the technique and details of the Code of Discipline which he or she is expected to follow during the ten days. In chapter 1 a passage from the Introduction is quoted which stresses that the teaching (*Dhamma*) 'is a universal remedy for universal problems and has nothing to do with any organized religion or sectarianism'. The Introduction goes on to explain very briefly, in simple terms which do not require any prior knowledge of meditation or of Buddhism, what *vipassanā* is and what it is good for, specifying that 'it is an art of living which frees the individual from all the negativities of mind such as anger, greed, ignorance, etc.', and 'a practice which develops positive, creative energy for the betterment of the individual and of society'. It then explains that

Vipassana meditation aims at the highest spiritual goals of total liberation and full enlightenment. Its purpose is never simply to cure physical disease, but as a by-product of mental purification many psychosomatic diseases are eradicated. Actually, Vipassana eliminates the three causes of all unhappiness – craving, aversion and ignorance. With continued practice, the meditation releases the tensions developed in everyday life and opens the knots tied by the old habit of reacting in an unbalanced way to pleasant and unpleasant situations.

The Code of Discipline is based on the eight precepts traditionally observed in Buddhist retreats, as already described above (section 2.2.2.1) in connection with Mahāsi Sayadaw's courses. In addition, in order to ensure maximum continuity in the exercise of unbroken mindfulness, avoiding distractions as strictly as possible, all participants are required to observe complete silence from the beginning of the course until the morning of the last day. This is known as 'noble silence' and is defined as 'silence of body, speech and mind'. This means that not only speaking but any other form of communication, e.g. by means of physical gestures, writing notes, etc., is to be avoided. Each student must concentrate unremittingly on his or her own practice. Students may, however, speak with the teacher whenever necessary (and are, in fact, interviewed from time to time to check on progress and any problems arising), and they may also, of course, speak to whoever is in charge of administration if it is essential in connection with any practical arrangements or necessities, but keeping always all contacts to an absolute minimum. In addition, students are instructed not to leave the site of the course for the whole of its duration, nor are any contacts with the outside world permitted (e.g. telephone calls, letters or visits) except in emergencies.

The working day begins at 4 a.m. and ends between 9.30 and 10 p.m., being entirely devoted to practice, with suitable intervals for food and rest. It comprises some eleven hours of meditation, alternating periods of individual practice and group sessions under the direct guidance of the teacher. In addition, every evening there is a talk by the teacher lasting one hour or more in which he provides all necessary information and instruction about various aspects of the teaching and the practice, at the end of which students have an opportunity to ask questions. Students are also free to seek individual interviews with the teacher and a period is set aside for this purpose every day.

3.3.2.2 Practical Exercises

Days 1 and 2

These are entirely devoted to mindfulness of breathing.[224] The student sits in a comfortable position, preferably crosslegged (but not

145

necessarily; what is important is to be able to hold the position for a good length of time). During the first three days the position may be changed if it becomes too uncomfortable, but not any more often than strictly necessary. The eyes are kept closed throughout all exercises. Breathing through the nose with mouth closed, the student concentrates on the feeling of the air as it goes in and out. At this stage the area of observation includes the whole inside of the nose, the nostrils and the upper lip below the nostrils. It is essential to remain strictly within this area, disregarding any other points connected with the act of breathing such as the throat, chest or diaphragm.

Thus one sits quietly, alert but not tense, following each in-breath and out-breath uninterruptedly from beginning to end. One observes the sensations, whatever they may be: tactile sensations of airflow, temperature, intensity and duration of each breath, etc. One endeavours to be as accurately and fully aware as possible of the precise quality of each sensation, but never attempts to induce or imagine any particular sensations. If, as can happen at the beginning, no distinct sensation is perceived, the student should not worry but simply note *blank* and persevere calmly. The absence of sensation is also an experience and one should be aware of it as such. When there is sensation, the student observes exactly *where*: inside the nostrils or at the openings, right side or left or both, in just one spot or in several places or all over. One is aware of any variations: airflow stronger or weaker, smoother or rougher, short or long. But always allowing the breath to come naturally, without forcing it or interfering with it in any way.

Any distraction arising through sensory stimuli (other than those produced by the act of breathing in the specified area) or from mental or affective sources should immediately be cut short by noting it mentally, so as to be clearly aware of its occurrence, and returning at once to the breathing (as explained in chapter 6, sections 2.4 and 2.5.2.1, in connection with the contemplation of the mind and of mind contents as subsidiary exercises).

Day 3

Continued practice of mindfulness of breathing, but narrowing down the area of awareness to the tip of the nose only (i.e. the edges of the nostrils) and the part of the upper lip just below the nostrils. The purpose of this is to strengthen and refine concentration by focusing more powerfully on a more restricted area.

Day 4

Begins with mindfulness of breathing as on Day 3, but after some time the student moves on to the full practice of *vipassanā*, with *contemplation of the body* as the primary exercise. To this end, the first step is to direct awareness *only* to the segment of upper lip below the nostrils (excluding the nostrils themselves). With the mind thus further concentrated on that one spot, one ceases to concentrate one's attention on the sensations caused by the breathing process and focuses on observing whatever intrinsic sensations (those not produced by the touch, temperature, movement, etc., of the airflow) arise in that same spot on which one has been focusing, i.e. the centre of the upper lip. This is the moment of transition from the contemplation of breathing alone to the contemplation of the body as such and of the sensations arising therein (which, as will be remembered, are the first two foundations of mindfulness explained in chapter 6, sections 2.2.1.3 and 2.3). If no sensation becomes apparent at first, mentally note *blank* and go on just keeping awareness there. If concentration is adequate there will be no shortage of intrinsic sensations to observe. We know well enough, from what scientists tell us, that our organism is in a constant effervescence of innumerable biological, chemical and electrical processes (such as blood circulation, the metabolism of body tissues, the impulses that travel along the nervous system, and so on) and that many other events occur at molecular, atomic and subatomic levels. All this we know intellectually, but it remains normally below the threshold of perceptual awareness in our everyday life, as the mind pursues its conscious, mainly outward-oriented concerns. What one now endeavours to do is to become clearly and consciously aware of these normally subliminal phenomena through direct experience.

At the beginning it is of course the rougher or more intense phenomena which are more easily perceived, such as tingling or pulsating sensations, changes of temperature, etc., in that small area of the upper lip. Whatever it may be, one should just observe it with the greatest possible clarity and precision, without reacting and without allowing one's mind either to start speculating about what is being observed or to wander off on irrelevant trains of thought.

Once attention has been concentrated and stabilized on the perception of intrinsic events and processes occurring on the upper lip, the student is ready to proceed to the methodical contemplation of the whole body. This is always done for the first time in a group sitting, under the close guidance of the teacher. The focus of concentrated attention is directed away from the upper lip and to the top of the head. The student then concentrates on the new spot for some time until the perception of intrinsic sensations is established (as previously on the upper lip). Then the student begins to scan the body from head to toes, moving methodically from one part to the next, without omitting any, paying precise attention to whatever sensation is present at that time. One should never try to imagine or induce sensations but just observe what is there. If no sensation is perceived, one should note *blank* and move on, mindfully and unhurriedly. As the scanning sequence is repeated again and again it will be found that awareness improves and previously blank spots also come to life.

On the first occasion (and the next few times, until the student is quite familiar with the technique) the scanning sequence takes place following detailed, step-by-step instructions by the teacher. In order to increase its impact and effectiveness as a combined exercise in both close attention and non-reactiveness, this first session of contemplation of the body lasts for two hours without interruption, and is undertaken with 'strong resolution' (*adhiṭṭhāna*). This means that, whatever position one takes up, one should resolve to maintain it without moving at all for the whole two hours, no matter how intense the discomfort that may develop. This provides an excellent opportunity to contemplate mindfully and equanimously the sensations arising in the body, which in the case of beginners become usually quite intense after some time of complete immobility, e.g. aches and pains, numbness, etc. When discomfort arises in this way the student is instructed to note the pain, etc., with detachment as one more sensation and, above all, not to move in order to ease it. In this way one comes to realize, through direct experience, that even aches and pains which seem quite intense to begin with are neither permanent nor unchanging, and one notices that, like all other bodily sensations observed, they tend to fluctuate, change and disappear (see in this connection what was said about the 'Compendium of Practice' in chapter 6, section 2.2.1.5).

The first unbroken two-hour *vipassanā* session is quite strenuous. New students do not always manage to keep it up for the full duration the first time. The psychological effect when one does achieve it, however, is remarkable – one feels one has broken through a mental barrier. By observing and accepting whatever arises, without clinging to comfortable sensations or pleasant thoughts and without resisting or trying to avoid pain or distracting thoughts, one gets one's first glimpse of the experience of acceptance which is of the essence of *vipassanā*.

From now on one tries to do all sittings in 'strong resolution', i.e. without moving, but each sitting, as a general rule, lasts not more than one hour at a stretch (although the more proficient students may, of course, hold the resolution for longer periods with profit).

The remainder of the day is devoted to further practice of the body scanning exercise, observing always the same sequence, from head to toes, alternating group sessions with individual practice.

Days 5 to 8

From now on one carries on improving and refining one's perception of phenomena as they occur by persevering in the contemplation of the body (practising always at the same time the observation of mental states and mental contents whenever they emerge, as indicated under Day 1, in order to maintain the unbroken continuity of attention). The basic method consists in the scanning of the body as described, but variations in the sequence and focusing are introduced in successive stages: surface scanning and depth scanning (alternating or combined), reverse scanning (i.e. from head to toes and from toes to head, instead of, as initially, always in the same direction), simultaneous awareness (i.e. scanning the body by groups of parts, e.g. both arms together, chest and back, both legs). From time to time the speed of the exercise – sometimes a slow scan, sometimes a rapid sweep – and the sequence in which the parts of the body are taken may also be modified at will (provided always that no part is omitted). As can readily be appreciated, the point of introducing variations is to make the exercise as comprehensive and full as possible, and to help in maintaining maximum vigilance by counteracting any dullness of mind due to excessive monotony.

Thus the student carries on trying (but always without tenseness, as trying too hard is self-defeating) to refine and enrich his or her perception of bodily sensations while maintaining instant awareness of any straying of the mind. Working always towards the fullest awareness, at the finest possible level, of all body and mind processes.

In addition, students are urged to make every effort to maintain a mental attitude of deliberate, mindful attention in whatever activities they have to engage in during the day, outside formal meditation periods. That is to say that while eating, when rising in the morning or going to bed in the evening, when walking back and forth, when washing, dressing, etc., they should practise, as subsidiary exercises, the *mindfulness of the postures of the body* and *clear comprehension of every action* (as seen in chapter 6, sections 2.2.2 and 2.2.3). These exercises are not only beneficial in themselves but also make it easier to get back to a more concentrated level of attention when one goes back to the main exercise in the formal sessions.

Effectiveness of the Method

At this point it may be useful to recall once again how insight gradually develops, and to outline the kind of psychological mechanisms involved, using for this purpose, as far as possible, contemporary Western terminology. This, of course, not in order to explain away the 'purification of the mind' of the Buddha's teaching by reducing it to nothing more than a kind of psychotherapy, but in order to facilitate our conceptual grasp of what is involved by reformulating it in more familiar terms.

The essential point to bear in mind is that the achievement of insight depends on the development of both *mindfulness* and *equanimity*, or non-reactiveness, and that both qualities are equally important. Let us briefly recapitulate:

Mindfulness, applied to the unremitting observation of all bodily sensation (from the most intense to the most elusive), results in the actual experience (as distinct from purely intellectual understanding) of the body as a pattern of continually changing phenomena (often perceived, at the subtler levels, as pulses or vibrations), i.e., in the terminology of modern physics, a web of high-energy events, each lasting for infinitesimally brief periods and interacting at unimaginably high speeds and frequencies. This is the experiential knowledge of (in Buddhist terms) the impermanence (*anicca*) and lack of identity (*anattā*) of phenomena and, in consequence, of their essentially unsatisfactory character (*dukkha*). This is the insight process of *vipassanā*, which consists, basically, in bringing about this experience through the fully conscious awareness of sense data and mental processes which are normally subliminal.

Equanimity, as has been seen, especially in chapter 8, means looking at whatever comes up in the process of mindful inspection and accepting it fully, without reacting for or against; without attaching oneself to pleasant sensations or recoiling from unpleasant ones, but simply observing each and every one of them as – in the traditional phrase – 'a sensation among sensations'. It must be clearly understood that one must truly train oneself *not* to react. Repressing reactions that arise is useless, since the very act of repression already implies a desire, a volition ('I do not *want* to react'). When there is a reaction to the observation, this means that one is still identifying with the experience. The correct strategy in such a case is not to repress the emerging impulse but to make at once the reaction itself the object of mindful, detached observation, thus disidentifying from it.

It will readily be appreciated that by not reacting one avoids generating the usual proliferation of feelings for and against, judgements, valuations and volitions – with their attendant strains and stresses – which normally accompany every experience, and which are in their turn sources of further reactions, emotions, thoughts, strains and complexes. This is the beginning of the purification of the mind. Whenever you maintain equanimity in the presence of sensations as they arise and pass away you are breaking the vicious circle. At these moments of mindful equanimity your mind is clean. In traditional terms, while in that state you are not accumulating new karmic consequences. What is more, whenever – thanks to the exercise of equanimity – your mind is not generating any new reactions then the strains, stresses, complexes, etc. (i.e. the karmic consequences), accumulated from earlier times start rising up from the subconscious or unconscious levels of the psyche and emerge into consciousness. There they are perceived, not necessarily in their original forms, as mental states or contents, but – very often – rather through correlated bodily sensations. This means, to give a very simplified illustration, that, for instance, an old psychic trauma may become manifest as a sharp pain in a certain part of the body, or a stifling sensation, or a speeding up of the pulse, etc., without there being a conscious recall of the event which originally caused the trauma.

That mental conditions have physical correlates is clear to everyone in certain obvious cases (e.g. the effect of anger on blood pressure or of fear on heartbeat). It is also well known that deep-seated complexes can cause powerful physical effects (such as cases of hysterical paralysis), and the psychosomatic nature of many illnesses is being increasingly recognized. What needs to be appreciated in the present context is that *all* psychological states and processes appear to have their – sometimes extremely tenuous – physical correlates, and that these are perceptible in terms of bodily sensations through sufficiently developed powers of concentrated, mindful observation. The conscious perception of the physical event (provided always that it is equanimous, i.e. non-reactive) discharges the energy of the psychological root condition and thus, as it were, 'defuses' it.

There is an obvious parallel here with modern psychotherapeutic techniques, in which mental and nervous disorders are treated by causing unconscious mental contents to become conscious. An important difference, however, is that in *vipassanā* one does not need to know what particular mental content is being cleared, nor is there a specificity of physical correlates: an accumulation of psychic energy (which would otherwise remain active as a source of future psychological or psychosomatic conditions) is simply dispersed as it becomes conscious in the form of sensation and is not reacted to.

Stated thus baldly, the suggestion that tensions of the psyche are discharged through correlated bodily sensations may appear rather oversimplified, but this is, of course, only a broad outline of the mechanism. In traditional Buddhist psychology there are detailed and highly sophisticated accounts of this process in terms of mechanisms and levels of the human psyche which have only recently begun to be studied by Western psychology and which fall outside the scope of this book.[225] The important point for us is that, in practice, the technique works. But let us return to the ten-day course.

Day 9

At this point, and as a culmination of the whole process, the student is introduced to the practice of loving-kindness meditation (*mettā*). The mind, cleansed and calmed by the *vipassanā* exercises, is now turned towards all other beings in a spirit of loving kindness. After performing the by now accustomed *vipassanā* practice for some time, the student is urged to share with all other beings the calm and balance achieved through the exercise of mindfulness and equanimity:

As a glowing ember radiates heat, let the feeling of peace and goodwill flow from your whble body in all directions. Think of all beings – those near and dear to you, those that are indifferent and those that may be unfriendly; those you know and those you don't know; near and far; human and non-human, great and small; make no distinctions. Your fellow feeling, your loving kindness, goes to them all.

It will be noted that this is a regular exercise in the extension of loving kindness, as described in chapter 8 (which may now usefully be reread, carefully relating it to the context of the course described here).

From now on the student should make it a regular habit to perform a short period (five or ten minutes) of loving-kindness meditation at the end of each *vipassanā* sitting.

Day 10

This is a day for recapitulation and for preparing the transition back to everyday life. The vow of silence is lifted and final words of guidance and advice are addressed to the students. The most important recommendation is to persevere in the daily practice of *vipassanā* on one's own, so as to preserve and develop the proficiency acquired in the course (ideally, it is best to practise two hours a day, one in the morning one in the evening or at night), and also to gather together for sessions with other similarly trained meditators whenever possible (once a week, if it can be managed).

4 *Conclusion*

This, then, brings us to the end of this study of the foundations of Buddhist meditation as preserved in the most ancient traditions. I should not like to close, however, without insisting once again that meditation is an essentially practical matter. Reading about it is not enough; you have to get down to doing it. Of course, an adequate intellectual understanding of what it is all about is useful and necessary as a starting point. This is the reason for this book, and for the brief selected bibliography that follows, which may help the reader interested in seeking further information about the teaching of the Buddha. But it must never be forgotten that the whole point of this teaching is to make it clear that the power to remedy the unsatisfactoriness of the human condition lies in our own hands. In the Introduction I already quoted the Buddha's powerful injunction to this effect: 'Meditate, and do not be remiss, that you may not have cause to regret it later.' I should like to close with another quotation that makes this essential point again. It is a verse from the *Dhammapada*, the best known of all the ancient Pali scriptures (it has been translated into many languages with over thirty different translations into English alone), and the most popular and best-loved in all Buddhist countries:

A man who preaches many truths
but is too lazy to practice them,
is like a cowherd who counts
the cattle of others[226]

Let us, then, count our own cattle, each working on one's own and all helping one another along the way.

Abbreviations

The discourses of the Pali canon from which quotations are given are grouped together in the *Sutta Piṭaka* (*Basket of Discourses*), which is one of the three 'Baskets' comprising the whole of the canonical texts, the other two being the *Vinaya Piṭaka* (*Basket of Discipline*) and the *Abhidhamma Paṭaka* (*Basket of Systematic Doctrine*). The parts of the *Basket of Discourses* from which quotations are given are identified with the following abbreviations (in each case, the figure or figures after the abbreviation indicate, as appropriate, the book, chapter, discourse or section):

D: *Dīgha Nikāya* (*Collection of Long Discourses*)
M: *Majjhima Nikāya* (*Collection of Middle-Length Discourses*)
S: *Saṃyutta Nikāya* (*Collection of Kindred Sayings*)
A: *Anguttara Nikāya* (*Collection of Discourses in Numerical Arrangement*)

The following are three of the fifteen books that make up the fifth and last of the collections in the *Basket of Discourses*: Kuddaka Nikāya (*Smaller Collection*):

Dhp: *Dhammapada*
Ud: *Udāna*
Sn: *Sutta Nipāta*

Other abbreviations
VDM: *Visuddhi Magga* (*The Path of Purification*); see note 31 and Selected Bibliography, Ñāṇamoli Thera.
HBM: *The Heart of Buddhist Meditation*; see note 156 and Selected Bibliography: Nyāṇaponika Thera.

Notes

1. Pali (*pāli*) is the language in which the teachings of the Buddha were preserved and transmitted in the early centuries, first orally, and then in writing from the first century BC. It belongs to the Middle Indo-Aryan group of dialects spoken in various parts of north and central India at the time of the Buddha (sixth and fifth centuries BC) and related to Sanskrit – the language of erudition and poetry – in varying degrees. Pali itself seems to be a kind of *lingua franca* developed for the easier dissemination of the Buddha's teaching, a mixed dialect based on the common characteristics of the others, and especially on the language of the kingdom of Māgadha (roughly, the State of Bihar in modern India), which was one of the most important areas of the Buddha's activities.

2. This is sometimes also referred to as *hīnayāna* (small vehicle) to distinguish it from the later *mahāyāna* (great vehicle), a subsequent development of Buddhist doctrine and practice which, starting from northern India, extended over the centuries to Tibet, Central Asia, China and Japan. For a variety of historical and cultural reasons, *mahāyāna* – as it spread – developed many philosophical and ritual elaborations of, and accretions to, the straightforward simplicity of the original teaching.

3. Although recourse to ritual and ceremonial elements (extraneous though they are to the Buddha's teaching itself) is not uncommon in some forms of Mahāyāna Buddhism, especially in its Tibetan varieties.

4. *Code of Discipline for Vipassanā Meditation*, Vipassanā International Academy, 'Dhammagiri', Igatpuri 422403, Maharashtra, India, p. 1.

5. *D*.16.

6. *D*.16.

7. *M*.152.

8. *M*.63.

9. *Nibbāna* is the original Pali term. The form 'nirvana', which has gained common currency in English and other Western languages, comes from the Sanskrit. The actual meaning of 'nirvana', however, has long been clouded by misunderstandings and misconceptions in the West (the *Oxford English Dictionary*, for instance, includes in its definition the idea of 'absorption into the supreme spirit', which runs counter to everything that the Buddha taught). It is therefore preferable to abandon the word 'nirvana', with its by now inevitable load of erroneous connotations, and to return to the original term.

10. *D.*22.

11. *D.*22.

12. Buddhist psychology distinguishes *six* kinds of 'sensations': those perceived through the five bodily senses, plus 'mental sensations' (i.e. perceptions of purely mental objects, without any immediate physical base).

13. *M.*38.

14. According to the law of *dependent origination* (*paticca samuppāda*, often also translated as *chain of causation*), usually formulated as a series of twelve links, each of which is the condition of the next one, the root of the series being *ignorance* (i.e. the failure to understand the radical impermanence of all that exists). Briefly, 'it expresses the doctrine that all physical and psychical phenomena are conditioned by antecedent physical or psychical factors, and that the whole of existence can be shown to be an uninterrupted flux of phenomena. The doctrine also implies rejection of the idea of any permanently existing entity or ego, human or animal' (Trevor Ling, *A Dictionary of Buddhism*). There is an excellent study of this by the Swedish psychologist and Pali scholar Rune A. Johansson (see Selected Bibliography). The parallelism is worth noting between this view of everything that exists as a web of interacting processes (*not* entities) and the conception of the physical world in modern high-energy physics. According to the latter, the atoms composing the molecules of what we perceive as solid matter are made up of subatomic particles which themselves are to be seen, not as having any degree of solidity, but as 'dynamic patterns, or processes, which involve a certain amount of energy appearing to us as their mass. . . . Matter has appeared in [high-energy particle-scattering] experiments as completely mutable. . . . In this world, classical concepts like "elementary particle", "material substance" or "isolated object", have lost their meaning; the whole universe appears as a dynamic web of inseparable energy patterns' (Fritjof Capra *The Tao of Physics*, Shambhala, Boulder, Colorado, 2nd edn, 1983, pp. 78, 80).

15. *D.*22.

16. The two basic texts here are the *Great Discourse on the Foundations of Mindfulness* (*D.*22) and the *Great Discourse on the Elimination of Craving (M.*38).

17. A careful distinction needs to be made between the meaning of *samādhi* in Buddhism and in orthodox Hindu Yoga. In Yoga *samādhi* denotes the culmination of the meditative process, often referred to as a state of 'superconsciousness', in which – in the

words of a leading contemporary Yoga master – 'the sādhaka loses consciousness of his body, breath, mind, intelligence and ego. He lives in infinite peace' (B. K. S. Iyengar, *Light on Prānāyāma*, Allen & Unwin, London, 1981, p. 11). This, in the Buddha's teaching, corresponds to the higher levels of absorption (*jhāna*) which can be achieved through tranquillity meditation (*samatha*), and which – in the Buddha's own experience – were not found to lead in themselves to the definitive insight of enlightenment (see chapters 3 and 5). In Buddhism, on the other hand, *samādhi* means simply 'mental concentration'. This is, of course, an essential condition for the practice of meditation, but no more than that. 'Right concentration' (*sammā samādhi*), i.e. rightly practised concentration, is one of the eight factors of the Noble Eightfold Path which leads to the cessation of suffering (see below in this same section (3.4) and also chapter 4).

18. *S*.56.11.

19. Who call themselves 'transpersonal psychologists' because they pursue the scientific study of human experiences and states of consciousness which transcend the boundaries of the 'self' or 'personality' as defined in traditional Western psychology.

20. Terminology proposed by the American psychologist Charles T. Tart in his article 'Scientific Foundations for the Study of Altered States of Consciousness', *Journal of Transpersonal Psychology*, vol. 3, no. 2, 1971. See also the important anthology *Transpersonal Psychologies*, Routledge & Kegan Paul, 1975, edited by the same author (who himself contributed the Introduction and three chapters) and comprising contributions by various authorities on Zen, Theravāda, Yoga, Sufism, Christian mysticism and others.

21. D. Goleman, *The Varieties of the Meditative Experience*, p. 116. (See Selected Bibliography.)

22. See chapter 2, section 3.2.

23. This is something that all meditative techniques, of whatever tradition, have in common.

24. See section 2 above of this chapter.

25. Charles T. Tart, in the article mentioned in note 20 above. On this whole issue, which is of capital importance, the excellent study by Goleman (note 21 above) is essential reading.

26. See chapter 6, section 2.6, and chapter 7.

27. Section 3.3 of this chapter.

28. *Ekaggatā*, in Pali. Literally, 'one-pointedness'.

29. Sections 4.3.9.4 and 4.3.9.7 of this chapter.

30. Section 4.2 of this chapter.

31. *Visuddhi Magga (VDM)*, ch. IV, p. 125 of the Pali text, and p. 130 of the English translation by the Venerable Ñānamoli (see Selected Bibliography). Frequent further references to this text will be abbreviated by giving the page of the original Pali followed by the page of the English translation in brackets. The present reference would thus read: *VDM*, IV, 125 (130). The terminology of the passages quoted has occasionally been adjusted to correspond with that of the present work, for the sake of consistency.

32. Section 4.1 of this chapter.

33. The three characteristics of all constituted or compound things, which are in a state of continual flux: arising – present – passing away (*uppāda – thiti – bhanga*), where 'present' refers to the infinitesimal moment of poise between 'arising' and 'passing away'.

34. *VDM*, IV, 126 (130).

35. *Kasina*, a term of uncertain derivation, possibly related to the Sanskrit *krtsna* (whole, entire, complete). It is a technical term of Buddhist meditation and best left untranslated. It denotes a material object or element used as perceptual input to develop mental concentration for meditation, being in many cases a specially constructed artefact.

36. *VDM*, 123 (127) specifies 'the size of a bushel or the size of a saucer'. The old commentary to *VDM* explains: 'As regards the words "the size of a bushel", etc., it would be desirable that a bushel and a saucer were of equal size, but some say that "the size of a saucer" is a span and four fingers [which would be about 30 cm] and that "the size of a bushel" is larger than that.'

37. *VDM*, IV, 124 (128).

38. This is intended to convey a sense of brightness and transparency, *not* to suggest that one should try and imagine a fanlike shape.

39. Meaning that the meditator has achieved the *counterpart sign* of access concentration, which is no longer tied to direct sense perception (preliminary sign) or to perceptual memory (learning sign). See section 3 above in this chapter.

40. *VDM*, IV, 125 (130).

41. *VDM*, V, 170–71 (178).

42. By looking directly at any available flame, without interposing the screen with a round opening described before.

43. *VDM*, V, 171-2 (178).

44. *VDM*, V, 172 (179).

45. *VDM*, V, 175 (181).

46. That is, disregarding the surrounding material. *VDM*, V, 175 (181-2).

Notes

47. *VDM*, VII, 198 (206). *Bhagavā* (literally, 'fortunate', usually translated as 'blessed') is one of the basic epithets of the Buddha; *arahant* (literally, 'deserving' or 'worthy', sometimes also translated as 'holy') is the specific term for the person who has achieved the deliverance of *nibbāna*, and is best left untranslated in most contexts. This formula, like the next two (on the *Dhamma* and the *Sangha*) is a very ancient form of words going back to the time of the Buddha himself.

48. *VDM*, VII, 213 (230).

49. In the progress of insight there are four stages or levels (see chapter 6, section 2.6.1), and each one of these has two aspects: the moment of entry into the stage or level, and the subsequent establishment of consciousness at that level. In traditional terminology, entry is known as *path*, and establishment as *fruit* or *fruition*. *VDM* explains that 'four pairs of persons' and 'eight kinds of individuals' are simply alternative ways of referring to these levels 'to suit differing susceptibility to teaching' on the part of hearers. The 'four pairs' are 'taking them pairwise, the one who stands on the first path and the one who stands in the first fruition as one pair', and so on, and the 'eight persons', taking them individually, 'the one who stands on the first path as one, and one who stands in the first fruition as one', and so on (*VDM*, VII, 219 (237–8).

50. The concept of 'merit' (*puñña*) in Buddhism must not be misunderstood. It is not a matter of rewards or prizes awarded by some sort of divine judge, but of good deeds (mental, verbal or physical) producing good consequences (in terms of spiritual growth and maturity, and sometimes also of physical or material wellbeing) through the natural operation of the law of causes and effects (See chapter 6, section 2.6.1.2: 'The Round of Rebirths').

51. *VDM*, VII, 218 (237).

52. *VDM*, VII, 221 (240).

53. *VDM*, VII, 223 (242).

54. It should be clearly understood that 'faith' in Buddhism is something rather different from what is usually meant by 'religious faith'. In fact, the Pali word *saddhā*, frequently translated by 'faith', as in this quotation, would be more properly rendered as 'confidence' or 'trust'. In Buddhism there is no question of blind belief in truths revealed by some supreme godhead (either directly or through prophets), or of belief founded on an unquestioning acceptance of authority. Rather, what is involved is a reliance, trust or confidence in the good sense of what the Buddha taught, but subject always – as the Buddha himself forcefully insisted – to verification by one's own experience: 'Do not be satisfied with hearsay or with tradition, legendary lore or what has come down in your scriptures; nor with conjecture, logical inference or the weighing of evidence; nor because you prefer a view, after thinking it over, or because of the supposed ability of whoever tells you something; nor because you think: "the monk is our teacher". Only when you know for yourselves: "These things are unwholesome . . . and lead to harm and suffering . . ., and these things are wholesome . . . and lead to welfare and happiness", then you should abandon [the unwholesome things], then you should practise and dwell upon [the wholesome things]' (*A.3.65*). Buddhist belief is anything but blind faith.

55. Reborn in various kinds of possible 'heavens', i.e. forms of existence which may be much more exalted, blissful, subtle and long-lasting than our human lives, but which are no less subject, in the long run, to change and impermanence.

56. *VDM*, VII, 225 (243–4).

57. *VDM*, VII, 234 (252).

58. This ancient conception of the organism is strikingly close to the observations of modern biology and medicine. The terminology, of course, is different. *VDM* does not, for instance, talk about micro-organisms but, rather more picturesquely, about the 'eighty families of worms' which inhabit the body.

59. Future existence, in its turn, will have its own specific characteristics and a certain duration, at the end of which it will be followed by yet further lives in the endless round of rebirths (*saṃsāra*) which can only be broken by the deliverance of *nibbāna*. It should be clearly understood, however, that there is no question here of a soul which moves on from one mortal physical form to another while keeping its own essence or identity, since – as the Buddha taught – there is no such thing as a self-entity anywhere at any level. What is reborn in the next life is the fruit of the actions performed in previous existences (*kamma vipāka*). (See chapter 6, section 2.6.1.2; 'The Round of Rebirths'.)

60. *VDM*, VIII, 238 (256).

61. In the Buddha's experience the whole of the perceptible and intelligible universe is an intricate web of interacting phenomena, all of them compound in nature and mutually conditioned and conditioning. There is only one thing that is simple, not compound, not conditioned, and consequently not subject to change and decay: *nibbāna*. In this formula the unconditioned mode that is *nibbāna* is presented by way of negatives, i.e. by briefly enumerating what needs to be eliminated in order to achieve it. In fact, nothing positive can be predicated of *nibbāna*, precisely because it is not part of the world of compound, perishable things to which all our logico-verbal structures relate. (See chapter 7.)

62. *Virāga*, sometimes also translated as 'detachment' or 'dispassion'. However, the more literal phrase 'fading away' is preferable since it best conveys the double connotation involved: as, through insight meditation, one gains direct experiential awareness of the unceasing *fading away* of all phenomena, one's own attachment to them – which is the root of all suffering – gradually *fades away*.

63. *VDM*, VIII, 293 (317).

64. An Enlightened One is a Buddha, i.e. a person who has achieved perfect understanding through full enlightenment and devotes himself to teaching others. It must be remembered that the Buddha of our age did not claim to be unique in the history of humankind, but simply one of those beings who, from time to time, rediscover through their own unaided efforts the universal truth of the origin of suffering and its cessation – a truth which, as he explained, tends to be forgotten over the centuries until, in due course, another human being arises, achieves full enlightenment and again teaches the universal truth. There were other Buddhas before Siddhattha Gotama, and there will be others after him.

65. *VDM*, VIII, 239 (259).

66. *VDM*. VIII, 240 (260). There is an alternative traditional formula which comprises only thirty-one terms. In this, the brain is not mentioned separately, but is included in the category of 'bonemarrow' and defined as 'the lumps of marrow to be found inside the skull'.

67. *S*.54.1.9.

68. *VDM*, VIII, 284–5 (306–7).

69. *VDM*, XI, 347 (379).

70. *VDM*, XI, 343 (376).

71. Here the established awareness of repulsiveness is the *learning sign*. As this awareness becomes more penetrating and intense, it constitutes the *counterpart sign*.

72. The five states of mind which hinder the progress of insight: sense desire, ill will, sloth and torpor, agitation and worry, doubt (see chapter 6, section 2.5.1.1).

73. *VDM*, XI, 347 (379).

74. *D*.22.

75. *VDM*, XI, 348 (381).

76. *VDM*, XI, 349 (382).

77. *VDM*, XI, 370 (405).

78. *VDM*, IX, 296 (322).

79. *VDM*, IX, 297 (323).

80. *VDM*, IX, 297 (323).

81. For the practice of loving kindness towards a hostile person – obviously the most difficult to achieve – *VDM* suggests a whole range of mental strategies to do away with one's negative attitudes towards the 'enemy', such as mentally reviewing his good qualities; reminding oneself that he, or she, too, is subject to sorrow and suffering; giving the person a gift, or accepting one from him or her, because 'in one who does this the annoyance with that person entirely subsides'; telling oneself that one should follow the Buddha's own example of boundless compassion and loving kindness, and so on.

82. There is also a classification into nine stages which, however, differs only formally from the more common eightfold one. It simply subdivides the second absorption of the traditional scale into two stages, with consequent renumbering of the rest.

83. See chapter 4, section 1.2.

84. See chapter 4, section 1.3.

85. See chapter 4, section 3.3.

86. *D*.22.

87. Obviously, if one is truly concentrating on the breath, for instance, there is no room in the mind for anything outside the meditation subject itself, as long as full concentration lasts.

88. *VDM*, IV, 142 (148).

89. *Pīti*, frequently also translated as 'rapture'. Although certain stages of it are accompanied by bodily sensations (as explained in the next paragraph of the text), it is exclusively a *mental* factor, which, as the Venerable Nyānatiloka explains, 'may be described psychologically as "joyful interest" ' (*Buddhist Dictionary*; see Selected Bibliography).

90. *Sukha*, in its most general sense, denotes any kind of pleasurable, positive experience, either physical or mental. Thus it stands for 'whatever is pleasant', being the antonym of *dukkha*: 'whatever is unpleasant' (see chapter 2, section 3.1). It is a specific factor in the first three absorptions.

91. *VDM*, IV, 145 (151).

92. *VDM*, IV, 143-4 (149-50).

93. That is, the five kinds of happiness just described. They are not all necessarily experienced by every meditator and not always in the sequence as given. There is a wide range of individual variation in meditational experiences, depending on each person's character, mentality and circumstances.

94. On the first few occasions when access concentration is achieved it usually lasts only for a short time.

95. *VDM*, IV, 144 (150-51).

96. That is, free from the five hindrances. See note 72 above and chapter 6, section 2.5.1.1.

97. *M*.43.

98. Although particularly gifted individuals may be able to stablize attainment almost at once.

99. *VDM*, IV, 152-3 (158-9).

100. One usually speaks about 'entering upon' and 'rising from' a state of absorption.

101. See note 72 above and chapter 6, section 2.5.1.1.

102. That is to say, the intellectual activities of 'applied thought' (ideation or thought formation) and sustained thought' (reflexion, ratiocination) are not fine enough tools to apprehend the subtle states of abstractive meditation. 'Gross' (*olārika*) is a term frequently used in Buddhist psychology to denote the relative lack of subtlety and stability of a given mental state. Within the broad gamut of states that go from the total confusion and 'grossness' of a mind entirely dominated by desire, ill will and delusion to the total clarity and 'fineness' of *nibbāna*, each stage is 'gross' as compared to the higher ones and 'fine' as compared to the lower.

103. *VDM*, IV, 155 (161).

104. *D*.22.

105. *VDM*, IV, 158 (164).

106. That is, the state still involves elements of mental agitation and confusion. See note 102.

107. *VDM*, IV, 158-9 (165).

108. *D*.22.

109. *VDM*, IV, 164 (170).

110. *Applied* and *sustained thought* (already absent from the second absorption) and now *happiness* eliminated in the third.

111. *VDM*, IV, 163 (169).

112. See note 90 above.

113. See note 102 above.

114. *VDM*, IV, 164 (170-1).

115. *VDM*, IX, 317 (342-3).

116. *D*.22.

117. *VDM*, IV, 165 (171).

118. *VDM*, IV, 168 (175).

119. *VDM*, X, 327 (355).

120. *VDM*, X, 327 (355).

121. *D*.16.

122. *VDM*, X, 331 (360).

123. *D*.16.

124. *Ākiñcañña* means, literally, 'no-thing'. In translating it as 'nothing' it must be borne in mind that, as a term in the series of the absorptions we are now considering, it has a purely descriptive, psychological value, and must *not* be taken as a metaphysical concept. In other words, it does not denote an absolute 'nothingness' and is thus not to be equated with the conception of *śūnyatā* (i.e. the integral and definitive void understood as the ultimate reality) which has been current in Mahāyāna since Nāgārjuna (second century AD). Pragmatically, the 'sphere of nothingness' (or 'no-thingness', as some authors prefer to leave it, to forestall misunderstandings) which is reached in the seventh absorption is a state of awareness in which there is not even the 'consciousness of consciousness' which distinguishes the sixth absorption. It is worth noting that the great German Buddhist scholar Paul Dahlke, in translating the *Discourse on the Noble Quest* (*Ariyapariyesanasutta*, M.26), felt it necessary to coin the special term '*nichtet-washeit*' (not-something-ness) and to explain in a footnote that it was 'in no way identical with *nothingness*'.

125. *VDM*, X, 333–4 (363).

126. *D*.16.

127. This is a direct quotation from one of the Buddha's *Discourses* (*Pañcattayasutta*, M.102).

128. The *sign* for this meditation is 'peacefulness'.

129. See note 72, and chapter 6, section 2.5.1.1.

130. *VDM*, X, 335 (364–5).

131. *D*.16.

132. *VDM*, XXIII, 702 (824).

133. *M*.43.

134. See in this connection Goleman's excellent study *The Varieties of the Meditative Experience*, already mentioned in notes 21 and 25.

135. See chapter 4, section 1.2.

136. See chapter 3, section 5.

137. See chapter 4, section 4.3.

Notes

138. See chapter 4, section 4.6. Once a degree of insight has been achieved, these – and especially loving kindness – are also frequently cultivated as a specific exercise beneficial to oneself and to others (see chapter 8 and chapter 9, section 3.3.2.2, Day 9).

139. Chapter 4, section 4.1.

140. Chapter 4, section 4.7.

141. Chapter 4, sections 4.3.9 and 4.3.10.

142. Chapter 4, section 4.5.

143. Chapter 4, section 4.2.

144. Chapter 4, section 4.4.

145. *S*.1.2.3.6.

146. *M*.10 and *D*.22.

147. *M*.10 in *The Way of Mindfulness*, by Soma Thera, and *D*.22 in *The Heart of Buddhist Meditation*, by Nyānaponika Thera (see Selected Bibliography). Both are also to be found (without notes or explanations) in the complete translations issued by the Pali Text Society (mentioned at the end of the Selected Bibliography), *M*.10 in the *Collection of Middle-Length Discourses* and *D*.22 in *Dialogues of the Buddha*.

148. *M*.10.

149. The reference to 'a monk' does not necessarily mean that these exercises were reserved to ordained practitioners. Simply, the Buddha was here instructing monks, but there are numerous examples of lay persons practising exactly the same techniques under his guidance or that of his pupils.

150. *Dantabhūmisutta* (*M*.125).

151. The Buddha's *Discourse to Bāhiya* in *Ud* (*Bodhivagga* chapter).

152. See chapter 4, section 4.3.9.

153. Chapter 4, section 4.3.10.

154. As explained in chapter 4, section 4.

155. Interpreting the Pali term *parimukkham* ('about the mouth'), which they could make no sense of, as if it were a synonym of *abhimukham* ('in front of the mouth'), which is a common adverb meaning 'facing'.

156. Thus in *The Way of Mindfulness*, p. 68, and even in *The Heart of Buddhist*

Tranquillity & Insight

Meditation (hereafter abbreviated *HBM*), p. 132, n. 4.

157. When explaining the practice of 'mindfulness of breathing' in his courses (see chapter 9, section 3.3.2).

158. *VDM*, VIII, 273 (294–5).

159. In *HBM*, for instance, the word 'breath' is added ('Conscious of the whole (breath-)body, etc.', p. 118), following the old commentary, with the explanation that the meditator 'will endeavour to keep his mindfulness at an even level throughout all three phases of a breath's duration' (p. 110).

160. See *HBM*, ch. 5 – 'The Burmese Satipatthāna Method'.

161. Sections 3.3.1 and 3.3.2.

162. *HBM*, p. 110.

163. The Pali adverbs are *ajjhatam* and *bahiddhā* and mean exactly this.

164. *HBM*, p. 58.

165. Personal communication, August 1982.

166. The Buddha's last words, already quoted in chapter 1.

167. *HBM*, p. 60.

168. See chapter 4, sections 4.2 and 4.3.9.

169. Section 2.2.1.3 in this chapter.

170. Bhikkhu Khantipalo, *Calm and Insight*, p. 95 (see Selected Bibliography).

171. Just enough to see where one is going, without being distracted by extraneous sights.

172. On this and the following sections of body contemplation, see also chapter 4, section 4.3.9.

173. When going out to beg his food.

174. Chapter 4, sections 4.2, 4.3.9 and 4.5.

175. A truly neutral input leaves us indifferent. However, a moment's reflection will show that genuinely neutral sensations are very rare. There are very few experiences which are entirely free from positive or negative aspects, i.e. which do not involve the least degree of evaluation on the part of the experiencer. This is why, especially at the beginning, one concentrates on the exact identification of the pleasant or unpleasant response.

Notes

176. Of course, even a fully enlightened *arahant* will quickly withdraw his hand from the fire to avoid getting it burned. The fundamental difference lies in the fact that the *arahant* will not remove his hand instinctively, unreflectingly, but deliberately, because the reasonable thing to do is obviously to preserve the physical integrity of the organism as long as this is required to function. However, if there is a valid reason to keep the hand in the fire (e.g. to save another person's life), he will leave the hand there and (if he truly is an *arahant*) will do so calmly, equanimously, because he no longer experiences what is going on as '*my* hand is being burnt' but, more accurately, as an impersonal process in which a number of elements are undergoing certain changes. In scientific terms, for instance, it could be described as a process of chemical combination accompanied by development of heat and light.

177. *HBM*, p. 69.

178. Chapter 5, section 2.2.1.

179. All the terms in this passage denoting different mental states are technical terms in Buddhist psychology. Some of them are near enough in meaning to our own usage, and need no special elucidation. The others may be understood as explained in the old commentaries, as follows:

shrunken: indolent, lethargic, unenterprising. Under the description of 'sloth and torpor' this is counted as one of the five hindrances to mental development in the traditional classification (see note 72).

distracted: agitated, restless. Another one of the five hindrances, under the name of 'agitation and worry'.

developed: having attained both the formal and the formless absorptions.

undeveloped: ordinary state of consciousness, operating on physical sense data.

surpassable: basically 'undeveloped' in the sense above. As such, it is surpassed by the states of consciousness attained in the absorptions.

unsurpassable: states of consciousness attained in the absorptions.

180. See section 2.6.1.6 of this chapter, and chapter 9, sections 2.2 and 3.3.2.2.

181. This follows the illuminating analysis of this section of the *sutta* by the Venerable Nyānaponika in *HBM*, pp. 73ff.

182. *A*.5.193.

183. Compare section 2.2.3 of this chapter.

184. See section 2.6.1 of this chapter.

185. See chapter 5, sections 2.2 and 2.3.

186. In section 2.6.1.5 of this chapter.

167

187. *Discourse on Mindfulness of Breathing* (M.118). There is an excellent translation, carefully annotated and including also extracts from the old commentaries, by the Venerable Ñāṇamoli (see Selected Bibliography).

188. Literally 'a happiness not of the flesh', that is to say, a happiness which does not depend on the bodily senses.

189. *M*.109.

190. 'What is perception? Monks, there are these six classes of perception: perception of [visible] forms, of sounds, of smells, of tastes, of tangible objects and of mental objects' (*S*.22.56).

191. *S*.22.59.

192. In chapter 3, section 5, and also in section 2.5.1.1 of this chapter.

193. Quoted from entry on *Ariya-puggala* ('Noble Ones' or 'Noble Persons'). See Selected Bibliography.

194. *M*.118. See note 187.

195. See note 9.

196. Summaries of such views can be found in Trevor Ling, *A Dictionary of Buddhism* (see Selected Bibliography); L. de la Vallée-Poussin, *Nirvāna* (in French), Paris, 1925; E. J. Thomas, *The History of Buddhist Thought*, London, 1933, 1971.

197. *M*.2.

198. *M*.29.

199. *Ud*.8.1.

200. See chapter 5, section 2.3.

201. *Ud*.8.3.

202. Alternative derivations have been proposed, e.g. from the root *vṛ* (to cover): a covered fire, being deprived of air, goes out. Another derivation popular with ancient commentators is from *vana* (forest): *nir* + *vana* = 'without forest', i.e. without fuelwood. In all cases, the basic meaning is always the same: extinction of a fire.

203. *A*.8.12.

204. *A*.3.32.

205. T. W. Rhys Davids, *Early Buddhism*, p. 73; R. Otto, *Das Heilige* (1917), as quoted by F. Heiler in *Die buddhistische Versenkung*, Munich, 1922; Rune Johansson in

Notes

The Psychology of Nirvana (see Selected Bibliography). Johansson's work is extremely helpful for an understanding of *nibbāna*, being based both on an exhaustive textual analysis of the Pali sources and a sound knowledge of psychology (the Swedish author, who died in 1981, was both a Pali scholar and an eminent research psychologist).

206. *VDM*, IX, 320 (346).

207. *VDM*, IX, 310 (335). This formulation should be considered in the light of what was said on rebirth and on the various possible levels of existence in chapter 4, section 4.3.6, and in chapter 6, section 2.6. Depending on the positive or negative implications of the accumulated 'residue' of past actions, rebirth may occur at levels that are higher ('states of bliss') or lower ('states of misery') than human existence.

208. *VDM*, IX, 309–10 (335).

209. *Sn.*1.8.

210. *VDM*, IX, 325 (352–3).

211. See chapter 4, section 2, and chapter 6, section 1.

212. *HBM*, p. 103.

213. See chapter 6, section 2.6.1.

214. See chapter 6, section 2.6.1.5.

215. On the historical significance of Mahāsi Sayadaw and the Burmese method of insight meditation, see *HBM*, ch. 5.

216. *HBM*, pp. 85–6.

217. This whole section should be read in the light of the analysis of the foundations of mindfulness in chapter 6.

218. Venerable Mahāsi Sayadaw, *Practical Insight Meditation*, p. 3 (see Selected Bibliography).

219. ibid., p. 4.

220. Saya U Tint Yee, in a memorial lecture on the occasion of the eleventh anniversary of U Ba Khin's death, given at the Rangoon Centre on 19 January 1982.

221. John F. Coleman *The Quiet Mind*, Rider, 1971, p. 69.

222. *S.*1.2.3.6.

223. U Ba Khin, *The Essentials of Buddhadhamma in Meditation Practice*, pp. 9–11 (see Selected Bibliography).

224. See chapter 4, section 4.3.10, and chapter 6, sections 2.2.1.1 and 2.2.1.2.

225. These are set out in detail in the *Abhidhamma*, the section of the Pali canon which elaborates, at the philosophical level, the teachings of the Buddha as presented in the discourses, with particular regard to the psychological analysis of existence. The full text (most of which is available in English in the translations of the Pali Text Society) is complex and rather dry. There are, however, some good modern analyses of it, such as the *Guide through the Abhidhamma Pitaka* by the Venerable Nyānatiloka, Buddhist Publication Society, Kandy, 1971, and a particularly good general introduction to it by the Lama Anagarika Govinda in *The Psychological Attitude of Early Buddhism*, Rider, 1969.

226. *Dhp*.19. My own translation. Literally it reads: 'Even if he recites many texts from the scriptures/the man who, slothful, does not act accordingly/ is like a cowherd/ counting the cattle of others.'

Selected Bibliography

Ba Khin, U, *The Essentials of Buddhadhamma in Meditation Practice*, *The Wheel*, no. 231, Buddhist Publication Society, PO Box 61, Kandy, 1976.

Burns, Douglas M., *Buddhist Meditation and Depth Psychology*, *The Wheel*, no. 88–9, Buddhist Publication Society, Kandy, 1966.

Goldstein, Joseph, *The Experience of Insight*, Unity Press, Santa Cruz, California, 1976; Shambhala, Boulder, Colorado.

Goleman, Daniel, *The Varieties of the Meditative Experience*, Rider, 1978.

Johansson, Rune E. A., *The Psychology of Nirvana*, Allen & Unwin, 1969.

Johansson, Rune E. A., *The Dynamic Psychology of Early Buddhism*, Curzon Press, 1979.

Khantipalo, Bhikkhu, *Calm and Insight*, Curzon Press, 1981.

King, Winston L., *Theravāda Meditation*, Pennsylvania State University Press, 1980.

Ledi Sayadaw, *Manual of Insight*, *The Wheel*, no. 31–2, Buddhist Publication Society, Kandy, 1961.

Ledi Sayadaw, *The Requisites of Enlightenment*, *The Wheel*, no. 171–4, Buddhist Publication Society, Kandy, 1971.

Ling, Trevor, *A Dictionary of Buddhism*, K. P. Bagchi & Co., Calcutta and New Delhi, 1981.

Mahāsi Sayadaw, *Practical Insight Meditation*, Buddhist Publication Society, Kandy, 1971.

Mahāsi Sayadaw, *The Progress of Insight*, Buddhist Publication Society, Kandy, 1965.

Ñāṇamoli Thera, *The Path of Purification*, Buddhist Publication Society, Kandy, 3rd rev. edn, 1983 (references in the text are to the 1st edn, Semage, Colombo, 1964). This is the translation of *Visuddhi Magga* (see below).

Ñāṇamoli Thera, *Mindfulness of Breathing*, Buddhist Publication Society, 3rd edn, 1973.

Nyānaponika Thera, *The Heart of Buddhist Meditation*, Rider, 1962.

Nyānaponika Thera, *The Power of Mindfulness*, Unity Press, San Francisco, 1972.

Nyānatiloka, *Buddhist Dictionary*, Buddhist Publication Society, Kandy, 4th edn, 1983 (references in the text are to the 3rd edn, Colombo, 1972).

Rahula, Walpola, *What the Buddha Taught*, Gordon Fraser, 1959; paperback edn, 1972.

Soma Thera, *The Way of Mindfulness: The Satipaṭṭhāna Sutta and Commentary*, Buddhist Publication Society, Kandy, 4th edn, 1975.

Vipassanā: special commemorative issue of *Vipassanā Journal* on the twelfth anniversary of the death of U Ba Khin (Vipassanā International Meditation Centre, Hyderabad, 1983) – a 284-page volume including essays by U Ba Khin, S. N. Goenka and assistant teachers, as well as students' accounts and articles on special professional applications of *vipassanā*.

Visuddhi Magga: the fifth century meditation manual by Bhadantācariya Buddhaghosa, original Pali text (Pali Text Society, London, 1920, 1975). Translated by Ñāṇamoli Thera as *The Path of Purification* (see above).

Note

All the canonical texts referred to are available in the original Pali (transliterated in Roman characters) and in English translations (not annotated) from:

Pali Text Society
Broadway House
Newtown Road
Henley-on-Thames
RG9 1EN
England

Index

173

Index

Index

Islam, 112

Jainism, 144
Jaipur, 143
Japan, 10, 143
Jesuits, 144
Jesus Christ, 52
jhāna, 22, 24, 25, 28, 54, 56–73
Johansson, Rune, 118

Kabbalah meditation, 73
kamma, 40, 106, 117
kasinas, 32, 33–6, 46, 47, 54, 57–8, 61, 65, 67, 68–70, 74

Latin America, 142
learning sign, 30, 31–2, 34–5, 58
Ledi Sayadaw, Venerable, 137
light, meditation subject, 33, 35
limited space, meditation subject, 33, 35, 54, 58, 61
loving kindness, 49–53, 54, 57, 65, 118, 119, 120–4, 152

Maharashtra, 143
Mahāsi Sayadaw, Venerable, 127–30, 139–40, 145
Mahāyāna Buddhism, 10
Majjhima Nikāya, 12, 75
meditation: concentration exercises, 28–9
  definition, 9
  levels of concentration, 27–8
  samatha, 10, 21–5, 28, 45, 54, 56–73, 107, 114, 125–6
  signs of concentration, 29–32
  subjects, 32–55, 57, 65–6, 74
  in the twentieth century, 125
  vipassanā, 10, 11, 21, 23–5, 28, 45, 73, 74–111, 113, 125–53
Melo, Anthony de, 144
mental objects, contemplation of, 76, 92–102, 104, 111
metaphysics, 114
metempsychosis, 104
mettā, see loving kindness
Middle way, 18–20
mind: in Buddhist psychology, 88–9
  contemplation of, 76, 90–2, 110–11
  unification of, 29, 63, 64
mindfulness, 64, 67, 74, 150
  of the body, 43–5, 48, 57, 74–5
  of breathing, 43–4, 45–7, 48, 57, 75, 77–81, 84, 110, 111, 129, 139, 145–7
  of death, 41–3
  foundations of, 75–103, 108–11

Mingun Jetawan Sayadaw, Venerable, 128, 129
momentary concentration, 23, 24, 28, 74
monasteries, 85, 125, 126–7
moral discipline, 18–20
Moslems, 112
movement, awareness of, 84–6, 149

National Buddhist Association (Burma), 129
neither perception nor non-perception, 54–5, 71, 114
Nepal, 143
New Zealand, 143
nibbāna (nirvana), 14, 22, 26, 40, 43, 72, 103–8, 112–18, 121, 140
nihilism, 116
nirodha, 117–18
Noble Eightfold Path, 18–20, 38, 39, 76
non-return, 72, 103, 106–7, 108
North America, 141–2
nothingness, 54–5, 69–71, 114–15
Nu, U, 129
nutriment, perception of repulsiveness in, 47, 57, 75
Nyānaponika, Venerable, 15, 83, 89, 109, 125–6, 128

once-return, 106
Otto, R., 118

pain, 66, 101–2
Pali scriptures, 9–10, 78, 109, 127, 153
paradise, 107, 112
'paths', 109
perception, 96
  cessation of, 72–3
  counterpart sign, 31
  exercises, 28–9, 34–5, 43–7
  neither perception nor non-perception, 54–5, 71, 114
personality, five aggregates of clinging, 99–100
personality belief, 104, 105
physiology, cessation of functions, 72, 73
pleasure, 66
posture, 32–3, 34, 78, 131–2, 145–6
  awareness of, 84–6, 149
preliminary sign, 30
preparatory concentration, 27, 29–30, 58
psychic energy, 151–2
psychology: Buddhist, 88–9, 93
  transpersonal, 25–6
  Western, 152
psychosomatic illness, 151
psychotherapy, 51, 150, 151
purification, 103–4, 106–8, 151

175

Index

Rangoon, 127, 129, 136, 138, 141
realization, 103
rebirths, 104–6, 107, 108
recollections, 36–47, 74, 131
reflective exercises, 28, 29, 32, 36, 48, 50, 57, 74
reincarnation, 104–5
repression, 95
repulsiveness in nutriment, 47, 57, 75
reviewing, absorptions, 61–2
Rhys Davids, T. W., 118
rules and rituals, attachment to, 104

Sagaing, 128
Sakādāgami, see once-return
Samādhi, see concentration
samatha (tranquillity meditation), 10, 21–25, 28, 45, 54, 56–73, 107, 114, 125–6
Sangha, 36, 38, 67
Sāriputta, 73
Satipatthāna Sutta, 75
Sayama, Mother, 142
seclusion, 63
self, five aggregates of clinging, 99–100
sensations: cessation of, 72–3
   contemplation of, 76, 88–90, 110–11
sense-bases, 92–3, 95–7
sense desire, 58–9, 93–5, 116
sensory input, 29
seven factors of enlightenment, 92, 97–9
Shelburne Falls, 143
signs of concentration, 29–32
singleness of mind, 63, 64
sitting meditation, 85, 86, 102, 110, 130, 132–5
six sense-bases, 92–3, 95–7
sotāpanna, 104
Soto school, 10
soul, reincarnation, 104–5
Southeast Asia, 10, 85
space: boundless, 54, 68–9, 70, 114
   ten directions of, 122
Sri Lanka, 10, 30, 80, 129
stream entry, 104, 108–9
subjects of meditation, 32–55, 57, 65–6, 74
sublime states, 49–54, 57–8, 65–6, 67, 74, 119–24
substrata of existence, 116–17
suffering, 14–18, 101–2, 113, 118
Sufi meditation, 73
sukkha vipassanā, 24

sustained thought, 59, 67
sympathetic joy, 49–50, 53, 57, 65, 118, 119

ten defilements, 116–17
ten directions of space, 122
ten recollections, 36–47, 74, 131
Thailand, 10, 80, 126–7, 129
Thathana Yeiktha, 127, 129, 130–35
Theravāda, 10
Thet Gyi, Saya, 137, 138
thought: applied, 59, 67
   sustained, 59, 67
'Three Jewels', 36–8
'Three Refuges', 36–8
Tibet, 10
Tint Yee, Saya U, 138
total-immersion courses, 138, 144
touch, perception exercises, 46
transmigration of souls, 104–5
transpersonal psychology, 25–6
truth, Four Noble Truths, 14–18, 37, 76, 92–3, 101–2

unification of the mind, 29, 63, 64
unworldly sensations, 90
upekkhā, see equanimity

Vedānta Hinduism, 112
vipassanā (insight meditation), 10, 11, 21, 23–5, 28, 45, 73, 74–111, 113, 125–53
Vipassanā Association of the Accountant General's Office (Burma), 138
Vipassanā International Academy, 143
Vipassanā Meditation Center, Shelburne Falls, 143
virāga, 117
virtues, 38–9, 49–54, 67
visual subjects, 32
visualizations, 29, 35, 45
Visuddhi Magga, 30, 31, 34, 36–7, 39, 41, 43, 44, 47, 48–9, 51–2, 58–68, 70–72, 80, 103, 121–2, 123–4

walking meditation, 32–3, 85–6, 87, 110, 130, 135
water, meditation subject, 33, 35, 47–9
wisdom, 18, 19–20
wordly sensations, 90

Yoga, 46, 73, 79

Zen, 10